D1256236

DATE DUE

SCIENCE

on the

ICE

SCIENCE
on the
ICE

An Antarctic Journal

Rebecca L. Johnson

Lerner Publications Company • Minneapolis

Research for this book was funded by a grant from the National
Science Foundation's Antarctic Artists and Writers Program.
I wish to thank the members of NSF's Division of Polar
Programs, particularly Guy Guthridge, for their encouragement
and support of my work in Antarctica. I am also indebted to
the many scientists who patiently answered my questions,
involved me in their research projects, and made me feel so
welcome in their field camps.

Library of Congress Cataloging-in-Publication Data

Johnson, Rebecca L.
      Science on the ice : an Antarctic journal / Rebecca L. Johnson.
        p. cm.
      ISBN 0-8225-2852-5
      1. Antarctica—Juvenile literature. [1. Antarctica.] I. Title.
    G863.J64 1995
    919.8'904—dc20   94-41487
                                                              CIP
                                                               AC

Manufactured in the United States of America
1 2 3 4 5 6 – I/JR – 00 99 98 97 96 95

Contents

1 Journey to the Bottom
of the World   7

2 McMurdo   17

3 Survival School   27

4 Weddell Seals   39

5 The Hole in the Sky   51

6 Going Fishing   63

7 Under the Ice   73

8 The Dry Valleys   85

9 The South Pole   99

10 Cape Bird   111

Index   *126*

Buried under ice and isolated at the bottom of the world, Antarctica remains one of our last wild and largely unexplored frontiers.

Chapter 1
Journey to the Bottom of the World

Crammed together in the front end of a military cargo plane, scientists and support staff endure the long, cold, noisy flight from New Zealand to McMurdo Station, Antarctica.

Snuggling deeper inside my parka, I tried to stretch my legs without waking the bearded man sitting across from me. Our knees—well padded in thick, insulated pants—were nearly touching. So were the knees of all the other passengers. We were crammed together like sardines near the front end of this military transport plane, a U.S. Air Force C-141 Starlifter. Beyond the people, the shadowy cargo area was packed full too. There were wooden crates of food and supplies, tarp-covered boxes of scientific equipment, machine parts, a few snowmobiles, and what looked like part of a helicopter.

Most of my fellow passengers were sleeping or reading—anything to pass the time on this five- to six-hour flight. We couldn't talk over the roar of the engines. It would be two more hours before we landed at McMurdo Station, Antarctica. At least that was the plan. But if a blizzard blew up around McMurdo, the pilot would be forced to turn the plane around and fly back to Christchurch, New Zealand. Boomeranging, it was called. We had already done that once. This was our second try for "the Ice."

7

No one lives in Antarctica permanently. Most people who visit are scientists who come to learn more about Antarctica's environment, wildlife, and history, and the impact this continent has on the rest of the planet.

I looked down the line of people, wondering who they were and what they would all be doing once we reached the continent. In the past, Antarctica was a destination for adventurers, explorers, and seal and whale hunters. These days, most of the people who spend time on the world's southernmost land are involved, one way or another, with science.

Biologists come to learn how Antarctica's wildlife survives extreme cold and is affected by changing environmental conditions. Astrophysicists and astronomers come to study the ozone hole, cosmic rays, stars, and meteorites. Paleontologists arrive in search of the fossils of dinosaurs and other ancient animals that once lived on the continent, while geologists study rocks to discover more about the formation of Antarctica and its relationship to the other continents. For glaciologists, Antarctica is one of the best places on earth to study ice, in all its many shapes and forms. Glaciers and ice sheets hold clues to changes in the earth's atmosphere and climate over long periods of time.

Scientists drill through the sea ice near McMurdo to study the ocean below (above). *Emperor penguins parade past a scientist* (right).

Along with scientists come support staff—teams of people who help scientists carry out their work and who maintain Antarctic research stations. Some are engineers, plumbers, and electricians, while others work as computer technicians, survival-school instructors, and heavy-equipment operators. The military lends a hand to scientists in Antarctica by transporting people, equipment, and supplies, and by helping with communications, weather forecasting, and medical care.

Glacial geologists study glacial deposits in remote locations.

The plane lurched suddenly, jarring the sleepers awake. But the constant droning of the engines soon had them dozing again. I closed my eyes and thought about Christchurch, where it was warm and green, and where this long journey south had begun.

———————

Special polar survival gear is a must for surviving Antarctica's fierce winds and subzero temperatures. The secret to warmth is wearing multiple layers of clothing.

"Be sure your boots are big enough," said a woman sitting on the floor, surrounded by heaps of clothing. She had been watching me struggle into a pair of white, lace-up rubber boots. "If they're too tight, it doesn't matter how many pairs of wool socks you wear, your feet'll still be cold." We were in the changing room of the CDC, or Clothing Distribution Center, in Christchurch. Everyone traveling to Antarctica with the United States Antarctic Program gets outfitted here with a complete set of cold-weather survival gear.

My pile of gear was considerable. And I had to try on everything, all together, to make sure it all fit: thermal long johns, windproof pants with a heavy insulating liner, a thick wool shirt, a down vest, a massive bright-red down parka, and two pairs of wool socks inside the funny-looking, but really warm, white rubber boots. Everyone calls them bunny boots. They have air bladders in the sides, with little valves to seal them off. The trapped air acts as extra insulation.

There were also several types of gloves and mittens, including a pair of gigantic bear paws mitts, along with a neck gaiter, face mask, cap, and goggles. With all those clothes on, I could hardly move.

Several days later, I was wearing most of my polar survival gear as we waited to board the C-141 for the second time. We had boomeranged the day before. Now we were ready to try it again.

It was a beautiful morning in Christchurch, warm

and sunny, with flowers blooming along the runway. Everyone was sweating under many layers of wool and down. Mittens, caps, extra cold-weather gear, water, and some high-calorie snacks were stashed in each person's only piece of carry-on baggage: a bright orange survival bag. One by one, we each picked up a sack lunch and a pair of foam earplugs and then stepped into the dimly lit interior of the plane.

Antarctica is the coldest place on earth. We would be arriving on the continent in early October, which is spring in the southern hemisphere. At that time of year, temperatures around McMurdo range between –10° and –30° F. Temperatures inland are much colder, down to –50° or –60° F. Add ferocious winds to that kind of cold—gusts up to 125 miles per hour—and you can have a truly life-threatening environment.

Scientists and support staff board a C-141 Starlifter plane bound for McMurdo Station. These and other types of military transport planes carry people, supplies, and equipment between New Zealand and the Ice.

Inside, people took their places quickly, settling down into the canvas bench-type seats, stowing their survival bags beneath them, and strapping in with heavy-duty seat belts. The loadmaster, a member of the flight crew, shouted out directions. "Pack in!" "Stow your gear *all the way* under your seat!" "Women up front!" He was wearing a headset to communicate with the pilot up on the flight deck. I pressed the foam earplugs into tiny rolls and pushed them into my ears. As the foam expanded, the deafening roar of the engines dimmed to a low growl. "Check your boots!" someone shouted. I made sure that the valves on my bunny boots were open. If the valves are closed, a rapid change in air pressure inside the plane can cause the boots to explode.

We sat on the runway for half an hour. Finally the plane began to move. The noise of the engines changed to a high-pitched whine as we taxied, faster and faster. Slowly, almost grudgingly, the C-141 lifted off the ground. We were on our way south again.

———

From the air, you can see how Antarctica is literally buried in ice. On the average, the ice cap is about 9,000 feet thick.

And so here we were, past the halfway point on our second attempt to reach the Antarctic continent. When the plane was about an hour out of McMurdo, I made my way forward and asked the loadmaster for permission to go up onto the flight deck. He spoke through the headset briefly, and then gave me the thumbs-up sign. I climbed up a short metal ladder into the cockpit. For a moment, I couldn't see anything but a blinding white light beyond the black shapes of the pilot and copilot. Gradually my eyes grew accustomed to the glare. Stretching to the horizon was a vast expanse of ice and snow with the tops of a few high mountains protruding from it.

For many minutes, I watched the icy landscape pass

Antarctica is a frozen desert that sits isolated and alone at the bottom of the world. It is a land of extremes—the coldest, windiest, driest, and highest of all the continents. It is as large as the United States and Mexico combined, yet all but a tiny fraction of the land is completely buried under hundreds of feet of ice.

Seeing all that ice, you might guess that it snows a lot in Antarctica. Along some parts of the coast, it does, but the interior of the continent receives less moisture each year than the Sahara Desert. Because it is so cold, most of the snow that falls inland doesn't melt. Over millions of years, layer upon layer of snow has collected on this polar desert to form an enormously thick ice cap.

Fewer than 100,000 people have ever set foot on Antarctica. No human being had even laid eyes on the continent itself until 1820. And it wasn't until the early 1900s that daring adventurers began to explore the interior. The South Pole was reached in 1911, and in the years that followed, many other remote areas were explored on foot and later by air. During the 1940s and 1950s, various countries claimed parts of the continent as their own and established Antarctic bases to protect their claims.

All of that changed in 1959, when the 12 nations that were most active in Antarctica signed an agreement known as the Antarctic Treaty. The treaty suspended all ownership claims and insured that from then on, human activities in Antarctica would be dedicated to peaceful research and international cooperation. Forty nations have now agreed to follow the treaty's principles. Today, Antarctica is a continent reserved primarily for science.

by underneath the plane. Here and there it looked pure white, flat, and featureless. But in most places there were ripples and crevasses, huge cracks that form as massive glaciers twist and turn around mountain peaks. After a while, the copilot caught my eye and jerked his thumb toward the rear of the plane—it was time for me to go.

I returned to my seat as the message "prepare for landing" was being passed down the aisles. On went parkas, neck gaiters, mittens, and caps. Gear was stowed. Seat belts were cinched up tight. I could feel the tension mount. There was a mixture of apprehension and excitement on people's faces. Everyone was awake.

We weren't going to be landing on a regular runway, but on the frozen surface of the sea near McMurdo Station. The C-141 began a long, slow descent that went on and on. The plane shuddered and lurched as it was tossed around by high winds.

Just when it seemed we must be about to crash right into the ice, we were thrown back in our seats as the plane pulled up hard and lumbered skyward. Fear showed on a few faces now.

The plane circled and then headed down again. Minutes ticked by. Finally, with a sudden jolt, wheels hit ice. The aircraft slid sideways, and everyone was thrown hard to one side. If we had not been tightly strapped in, we all would have been piled up on one side of the plane like so many matchsticks. After that, the plane straightened out and taxied smoothly. There were a few cheers and some clapping. Lots of smiles.

The C-141 gradually slowed to a stop. After a few minutes, the door was pulled open. Dazzling white light flooded in. I put on my sunglasses and joined the scientists and other passengers as they got off the plane. Squinting against the brightness, I stepped down onto hard-packed snow and looked around. The plane had

landed in the middle of an enormous sheet of ice that stretched out in all directions. Misty gray mountains rose up in the distance on one side, while black volcanic hills loomed close on the other. We were here, breathing in the cold, clean air of Antarctica.

It feels wonderful to step onto Antarctic ice after so many hours in the air.

McMurdo Station is the largest scientific research station in Antarctica. Late in the summer, when the sea ice on McMurdo Sound softens and breaks up, resupply ships make a channel through the ice and dock near the shore.

Chapter 2

McMurdo

Survival bags in hand, we crunched across the dry, hard-packed snow that covered the sea-ice runway. It felt good to walk again. And it was thrilling to think about where we were walking.

We made our way over to the edge of the runway, where several strange-looking vehicles were parked next to a cluster of small buildings. The vehicles had massive tires and were painted bright orange. Someone said they were called Deltas.

I climbed up a metal ladder into the back of one of the Deltas and sat down on a bench seat that ran along the side of the boxy compartment. Up in front, a heater was blasting out hot air. A few minutes later, packed with new arrivals, the monster truck started up. It rumbled slowly across the ice, following a route marked with red and green flags.

We were being driven across the frozen surface of McMurdo Sound, the part of the Ross Sea between Ross Island and the Antarctic mainland. On the left, looming very close, was Ross Island, the site of McMurdo Station and New Zealand's Scott Base. A mass of dark volcanic ridges and dazzling glaciers, Ross Island is dominated by Mount Erebus, an active volcano that rises

On its way to pick up new arrivals, a Delta follows the flagged route across the sea ice from McMurdo.

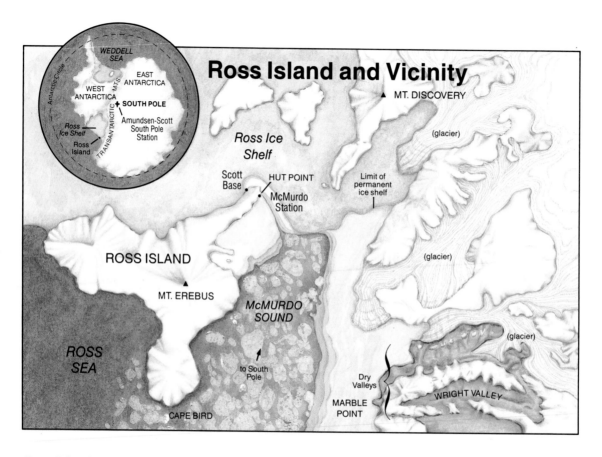

Ross Island and Vicinity

Ross Island lies just off the coast of the Antarctic continent. The body of water that separates the island from the mainland is McMurdo Sound. McMurdo Station and New Zealand's Scott Base are located on a peninsula on the south side of the island.

12,448 feet above the surface of the sea. Clouds of steam puffed out from its top as we passed.

Across the sound on the right were towering, glacier-covered mountains, part of the Transantarctic Mountain range that divides the continent into East and West Antarctica. The sun was just skimming the jagged tops of those mountains. It was strange to think that I would never once see the sun set during my stay. Because of Antarctica's position at the bottom of the world, there is continuous daylight during the summer and continuous night during the winter. At this latitude—McMurdo is at 78° south—the sun stays above the horizon from October through February. After that it begins to dip below the horizon, getting lower and lower in the sky each day. Around the end of April, it disappears completely, not to be seen again until late the following August.

The flagged route wound around a bit of land that jutted out from the island. As we rounded this point, McMurdo Station came into view. Buildings of various shapes and sizes sprawled along the shore, backed by low, dark hills. Scattered among the buildings were storage tanks, stacks of crates and cargo, and piles of snow made gray by black volcanic grit blown down from the hillsides.

The Delta slowed to a snail's pace as it reached the junction between the frozen surface of the sea and the island's shore. The sea ice was buckled and broken here, where tides and currents in the water below had pushed the ice up against the land. Slowly the Delta lurched across the rough ice and then drove up into McMurdo. There were a few people working outside, their faces covered by face masks and goggles, or hidden inside fur-trimmed hoods. Eventually we jerked to a stop outside a wooden building that looked like a ski chalet, and everybody got out. We clumped up the steps in our bunny boots and went inside. "Welcome to Mactown," someone called out.

The Chalet, which is the National Science Foundation's headquarters in Antarctica, is where all the new arrivals get their first introduction to life in McMurdo. During the next hour, we were given housing assignments and told about water conservation (only two showers a week!), fire safety, meal times, the recycling program, and a long list of other topics.

During orientation, I began to realize that Antarctica has a language of its own. "Mactown," for instance, is Antarctic slang for McMurdo. We were a new group of "pax," including many "beakers," who had just arrived from "Cheech." Quite a few other words and phrases

During the summer season, about 1,200 scientists, support staff, and military personnel live at McMurdo Station. Fewer than 200 people occupy the station during the long, dark winter.

This sign welcomes new arrivals to McMurdo Station.

Antarctic Slang

bag drag—the much-repeated routine of suiting up in all your cold-weather gear and hauling your bags to Hill Cargo prior to boarding an aircraft, only to be told that the weather has changed (again!) and all flights are canceled until further notice

beaker—a scientist doing research in Antarctica

Cheech—Christchurch, NZ

DV—a distinguished visitor; someone who gets special treatment while in Antarctica

freshies—eggs, fresh fruits and vegetables; anything that's not canned, frozen, or dried

helo—helicopter

hey, it's a harsh continent—quit complaining!

house mouse—what you are called when it's your turn to help with cleanup duties around a field camp or station

the Ice—Antarctica

pax—passengers

Pole—Amundsen-Scott South Pole Station

toast—a word used to describe what you become when you've been in Antarctica too long; i.e., "She's toast!"

winter-over—spend the winter in Antarctica

soon became part of everyday conversation down on the Ice.

My first stop after the briefing was Hill Cargo, a sort of big, metal Quonset hut near the center of town, where I retrieved the one piece of luggage that I'd been allowed to check on the C-141. After that, I headed off to find my room.

Most of the support staff in McMurdo live in large, modern dormitories that have central heating, carpeted rooms, bathrooms with showers, and laundry facilities. During times when the station is particularly crowded, some people are housed in old-fashioned shelters called Jamesways. They are long, low huts made of canvas stretched over a rounded wooden frame—a bit primitive and rather cold.

Most of the scientists live in small dormitories near the Chalet. I found my room in one of these, an older,

During my time in McMurdo, I lived in a drafty dormitory (lower right) *next to the NSF Chalet* (lower left). *The focal point for scientists is the Crary Lab* (center) *where they have their office space and laboratories.*

two-story wooden building. It had two bunk beds, a desk and chair, and a wardrobe. There was just one small window that looked out onto a row of small tracked vehicles lined up in the snow. The curtains on the window were heavy, to block out the sun during the night.

After I had unpacked a few things, I slipped on my parka and mittens and headed out into the streets of McMurdo. The station was established in 1956 as a military base. Over the years, some new buildings have been added, some old ones destroyed, and the result is a maze of historic sites and modern structures. Few of the buildings are identified on the outside, so it takes a bit of exploring to discover what's what.

A broad view of McMurdo Station shows the newer dormitories (left) *and the Crary Lab* (right).

Down near the shore, I found the power plant, which provides the station's electricity. The fuel burned to power the generators is a type of jet fuel, which is stored in huge tanks perched high on the hills overlooking the station. Next to the power plant is the water distillation plant. Seawater is pumped up from under the ice, and the salt is removed from it to make freshwater for drinking and washing. In Antarctica, freshwater is precious, and everyone is constantly reminded to use it sparingly. Water lines, sewer pipes, electric lines, and other utilities all run above ground.

Farther along the shore, I found the headquarters of VXE-6, the Antarctic Naval Air Squadron. Navy pilots and crews are responsible for transporting scientists and supplies to and from research sites, field camps, and the South Pole by airplane and helicopter. Not far from the VXE-6 is the helo pad where the bright red-orange navy helicopters take off and land.

Just behind the helo pad is Observation Hill, or Ob Hill for short. From the top, there is a wonderful view of the station, Mount Erebus, the sound, and the Ross Ice Shelf.

Near the center of McMurdo, I walked by repair shops, a library, a post office, a chapel, warehouses, heavy equipment storage buildings, a gym, several clubs, and the galley. In a way, the galley is the heart of McMurdo—it's where the food is. In addition to breakfast, lunch, and dinner, a midnight meal is served for people who are working through the night. Everything is served cafeteria style, and there are no limits on how much you can eat—not even on frozen yogurt! When you work outdoors in a place as cold as Antarctica, you burn a lot of calories just generating enough body heat to keep warm.

Enough food is stored in McMurdo to last almost three years. During the summer season, fresh fruits and

The Ross Ice Shelf, called the Barrier by some of the early Antarctic explorers, is a vast sheet of permanent sea ice that stretches hundreds of miles south of the island. It is roughly the size of France. A great wooden cross stands at the top of Ob Hill in memory of the Antarctic explorer Robert F. Scott and four of his companions. Scott and his men died on the Barrier in 1912, as they were returning from a terrible, ill-fated journey to the South Pole.

Scott and his four companions at the South Pole

Scientists and support staff gather for a meal in the galley.

Antarctica is the cleanest continent on earth, and keeping it that way has become a top priority. There are very strict rules about recycling and waste disposal.

vegetables arrive by cargo plane from New Zealand. Whenever bad weather prevents planes from landing for long periods of time, the freshies quickly disappear. Then the cooks in the galley must make do with only canned, dried, and frozen foods until incoming planes can resupply the station.

Every once in a while, during these fresh food shortages, a great mound of leaf lettuce will appear mysteriously in the galley. Hidden away in a tiny building on the edge of McMurdo is a hydroponics garden where lettuce, tomatoes, onions, and a few other vegetables are grown in water, not soil. During the winter, when McMurdo is isolated from the rest of the world for almost six months, the fresh food from the hydroponics garden is a wonderful treat for the people who winter-over.

One of the most interesting places in McMurdo is Mac Center, the navy-operated communications and weather center. Weather forecasting is very difficult in Antarctica, because conditions can change unbelievably

These vegetables are being grown in nutrient-enriched water in the hydroponics garden.

Antarctic Weather Conditions

Condition 3
- winds less that 55 miles per hour
- windchill warmer than −75° F
- visibility more than ¼ mile

Condition 2
- winds 55 to 63 miles per hour
- windchill −75° F to −100° F
- visibility 100 feet to ¼ mile

Condition 1
- winds greater than 63 miles per hour
- windchill colder than −100° F
- visibility less than 100 feet

The top photo shows the view from the window of my room in McMurdo during Condition 2. The bottom photo shows the same view during Condition 1.

fast. A team of forecasters at Mac Center uses information gathered by satellites, weather balloons, and remote weather stations to predict Antarctica's weather. Knowing what to expect from the weather is important for just about everyone on the continent.

The meteorologists at Mac Center rate the weather conditions on a scale of 3 to 1. A Condition 3 day is a nice day in Antarctica: cold, but "relatively calm" with good visibility. Condition 2 is much more common. If you need to travel outside the station when it is Condition 2, you must be in a radio-equipped vehicle and stay on the flagged routes. Helicopter flights usually are stopped when the weather drops from Condition 3 to Condition 2. Condition 1 is extremely dangerous, life-threatening weather, when winds are powerful enough to blow you over, windchills are low enough to freeze skin in just a few seconds, and the visibility is only a few feet, or less. When the weather is this bad, everyone stays inside the nearest available shelter.

It takes a while for new arrivals to realize just how dangerous the harsh Antarctic environment can be. Regulations that require you to wear your cold weather gear and carry a survival bag just to travel a few hundred feet beyond the station might seem silly and overcautious. But they aren't. Researchers have been working out in the field under clear skies only to find themselves in the middle of a howling blizzard less than an hour later. A typical Antarctic blizzard lasts three to five days with high winds and deadly windchills. As the wind whips the snow around, visibility may drop to zero. You may not be able to see your own feet, let alone a vehicle, hut, or any nearby landmarks. It can take rescue parties many days to reach people who are stranded or in trouble.

Most scientists working in Antarctica spend much of their time in the field. Once away from the relative safety of McMurdo, with its heated buildings, running water, and vast food and fuel supplies, researchers are face-to-face with the elements. So one of the first requirements after arriving in McMurdo is to learn how to survive on this harsh continent.

Windblown snow surrounds a remote field camp.

In survival school, you learn the basic skills needed to survive in the harsh Antarctic environment.

Chapter 3

Survival School

Ice climbing at survival school

Early on the third day after arriving in McMurdo, I reported to the Berg Field Center, along with a few scientists and support people, for my first survival class. The BFC, as everyone calls it, is the place where researchers are outfitted with equipment and supplies for their trips into the field. There were wooden sledges stacked in neat piles near the entrance, ready for cross-country expeditions. Inside were coils of rope, lines of skis, and heaps of snowshoes. Boxes of gear, from freeze-dried food to candles, filled shelves that reached to the ceiling. One entire room was filled with down sleeping bags and insulated pads. Our group was here for Sea Ice Training, a day-long survival class in which we would learn how to travel safely on the sea ice offshore.

Up on the second floor of the BFC, above all the supplies and gear, we met Tim Cully, our Sea Ice Training instructor. He didn't waste any time getting started. First, he told us all about ice, especially the types of cracks that run through it: straight-edge cracks, tidal cracks, spreading cracks…there was quite a lot to learn. Then, grabbing a very large red duffle bag that was propped up against the wall, he launched into a lecture

Sea Ice

Every winter, an immense pack of ice up to 10 feet thick forms on the sea around Antarctica. In some places, the pack extends outward from the continent for more than a thousand miles. During the summer months, however, warmer temperatures cause the sea ice to soften and melt, and the pack breaks up into countless pieces that drift around the coast, driven by winds, currents, and tides.

From April through early December, the sea ice that covers McMurdo Sound is fairly solid and thick enough—in most places—to support quite a bit of weight, even the huge aircraft that land on the sea-ice runway. But beneath the frozen surface of the sound, the sea is always moving. As it does, the ice cracks, twists, heaves, and buckles. Currents can also wear the ice away from underneath. Wherever sea ice is cracked or worn thin, it can be very dangerous to cross.

At the beginning of each research season, a few safe routes across the sea ice are marked with flags. But if you travel anywhere else on the ice, you must be extremely careful. What looks like thick ice might actually be quite thin—too thin, perhaps, to support you or your vehicle.

If you fell through the ice, your only hope of survival would be to get out of the water immediately. The temperature of the seawater in McMurdo Sound hovers around 28° F. In water that cold, the average person can last only about five minutes before losing consciousness.

Many of the tracked vehicles that scientists and support personnel use to travel around on the sea ice have escape hatches in the roof. If a vehicle breaks through the ice, the people inside may have a chance to get out through the top before it sinks. But that isn't always possible. The ice near McMurdo has claimed the lives of several people over the last 20 years or so. They died when the vehicles they were driving broke through the ice and sank before they could get out.

about the gear that we would need to survive if we were stranded out on the ice. "OK, everybody," he began, "whenever you leave McMurdo, you must carry one of these survival packs for every two people. That's in addition to your orange bag, with your personal gear." He started unpacking the bag, describing each piece as he spread the contents out on the floor.

The red duffle contained a two-person nylon tent, two sleeping bags with pads, a tiny portable stove, a cooking kit, fuel, matches, candles, packets of freeze-dried food, a first-aid kit, extra socks and mittens, a signal mirror, rope, a collapsible snow shovel, a snow saw, a survival manual, and a few comic books. Used properly, this was enough gear to sustain two people for several days in an emergency.

Tim demonstrated how to start the stove and how to take it completely apart, clean the valves, and put the whole thing back together again. Then he showed us how to put up the tent and tie a few basic knots. "What about the comic books?" someone asked. "The comic books," Tim said with a grin, "will give you something to read while you're huddled inside your tent waiting for a storm to pass or help to arrive." After that, we loaded enough survival gear for the group in a tracked vehicle called a Hagglund that was parked outside the BFC, and headed out.

Our first stop was Hut Point, a ridge of land on the edge of McMurdo that overlooks the sound. From this high point, we had a clear view of the sea ice and could easily see the cracks that ran across parts of it. Some

Sea ice covers the surface of McMurdo Sound for most of the year. Only during the height of the summer does the ice break up.

cracks close to land were large and jagged. Farther out, the cracks were smaller and less noticeable, and many were partly hidden under a thin covering of snow.

As we left McMurdo, Tim raised Mac Center on the radio and went through the standard check-out procedure. He reported that our vehicle, with "eight souls on board" was going out onto the ice and explained where we were going and when to expect us back. Mac Center then gave us permission to leave the station along with an update on the weather. Despite the cold, it was supposed to remain clear and relatively calm for the next few hours at least.

Heading north from McMurdo, Tim drove along a flagged route for awhile, and then veered off onto uncharted ice. After a few minutes he stopped and we all got out. Before going any farther, we had to make sure that the ice we were traveling on was thick enough to be safe.

"First you have to dig down through the snow to expose the surface of the ice," said Tim. We all helped do this while he brought out a hand-operated auger drill and extra drill-bit extensions, each about three feet long. With the snow cleared away, we started drilling. It's hard work to drill through solid ice by hand. Each person took a turn and worked the drill for several minutes and then let someone else take over. The ice in this first spot was very thick—we had to add two extensions to the drill. When the drill finally broke through to the bottom of the ice, a small geyser of seawater gushed up through the hole.

Tim dropped a meter tape that had a small metal bar attached to its end down through the hole. He let down several meters of tape, and then began slowly pulling it upward. When he felt the metal bar bump against the underside of the ice, he checked the tape: 220 centimeters. This ice was over seven feet thick, more than

Using a hand-operated drill, it takes about 10 minutes to drill through sea ice that is seven feet thick. A drill-bit extension is lying on the snow in the background.

twice the thickness necessary to support a Hagglund. So there was no problem right here.

And so we continued driving across the ice, stopping every few minutes to check out cracks and measure ice thickness. Near cracks, the ice was sometimes quite thin, and we were forced to take a different route.

Around noon, we stopped and ate lunch inside the Hagglund. Sandwiches thickly spread with butter, granola bars, trail mix, and chocolate bars were all washed down with steaming hot cocoa. Such a high-calorie, high-fat meal might not seem very healthy, but since we were working hard in a very cold environment, we were using up so much energy that it was a necessity. We also drank a lot of water. Antarctica is such a dry place that a person's body loses water very quickly, especially when working hard and sweating. To avoid getting dehydrated, it's necessary to drink at least a gallon of water a day!

Working in the shelter of a Hagglund, we put up a survival tent on the sea ice.

Cooking lunch at survival school, with Mount Erebus in the background

After lunch, Tim demonstrated how to put up the tent on ice. "If you're out here and get caught in a blizzard," he said, "your number one priority is to put up a shelter to protect yourself from the wind and cold. Don't stay in your vehicle. In Antarctica, anything metal gets fiercely cold. You'll be warmer in the tent."

Once the tent was up, we lit the stove and melted pieces of ice to make hot water. With a shelter from the wind, something warm to drink, dry clothes, fuel, and a little food, I probably wouldn't be comfortable, but I'd survive.

As we were repacking the tent and getting ready to leave, the wind suddenly changed direction. Fifteen minutes later, dark clouds appeared in the southern sky. Bad weather was coming, and it began to look like we might be putting our newly learned survival skills to the test very soon, unless we could reach McMurdo before the storm hit.

Once we reached the flagged route, however, we made good time. It wasn't until the Hagglund drove into the station that the wind really started to howl and the air filled with blowing snow.

The storm had blown over by the next morning, when survival school continued with two days of Snow Craft training. Tracked vehicles took our group out to a spot on the Ross Ice Shelf, about six miles from McMurdo.

For the first few hours, a team of instructors taught us the basic skills needed to build different kinds of snow shelters, from simple one-person trenches to igloos that would sleep half a dozen people. Our first assignment was to make wind breaks out of snow blocks. Using snow saws, we cut rectangular blocks out of the hard-packed snow and stacked them up to form curved, waist-high walls behind which we could do our cooking.

Once the wind breaks were finished, we got our

Unlike the sea ice, which melts and breaks up each summer, ice shelves are fairly permanent features in the Antarctic. The Ross Ice Shelf is several hundred feet thick at its northern, or outer, edge and over two thousand feet thick at its southernmost margin, where it meets the land.

At survival school, some people build igloos to sleep in overnight (left). Others pile up survival bags and shovel snow on top to make what will become a snow mound shelter (below).

instructions for the rest of the day: We each had to build some type of snow shelter. And to make this experience as much like a survival situation as possible, we had to spend the night in whatever we built!

After debating the options for a few minutes, I joined forces with a woman named Heather, and we started building a snow mound. Our first step was to pile up half a dozen survival bags and shovel snow on top of them. We shoveled and shoveled and shoveled, until the bags were buried under a thick layer of snow. Then, using the backs of the shovels, we pounded on the snow with all our might to compact it into a hard, strong shell.

After two hours, the outside of the mound was done. Heather and I took a break to heat water for a cup of hot cocoa and to eat chocolate bars for a quick energy boost.

Then came the hard part. Starting about three feet from the mound, we dug a tunnel through the snow that came up directly underneath the mound. Working in this narrow passageway on our backs, we broke through the bottom of the mound and pulled the survival bags out, one by one. Once the bags were all out, we were left with a hollowed-out dome of snow.

For several more hours, we scraped snow out of the inside of the mound until there was enough room for two people, plus gear. At 9:00 P.M., we stood back and surveyed our work. The mound looked great, but it had taken nearly five hours to build. Exhausted and hungry, we fired up our tiny stove behind the windbreak and heated enough water to make freeze-dried chili and hot orange drink. We ate standing up, with mittens on, stomping our feet and wriggling our toes inside our boots to keep our feet warm.

After we had packed away the cooking gear, Heather and I struggled through the tunnel into the mound and got ready for bed. I unrolled my insulated pad on

Two survival school participants cook dinner in the shelter of a snow trench.

the hard snow floor and laid my sleeping bag over that. I took off my boots and outer clothing and crawled inside my sleeping bag, still wearing long johns, two pairs of wool socks, a Polarplus pullover, a down vest, a neck gaiter, and the wool liners of my leather mittens. My last step was to pull the drawstring around the top of the sleeping bag and enclose my head in down.

A soft blue light filtered through the top of our shelter. It was very quiet inside, and despite the cold, I quickly fell asleep.

I woke up at 5:30 A.M. when the ice crystals that had formed around the hood of my sleeping bag during the night fell into my face. It took courage to crawl out of a warm bag and put on ice-cold pants, parka, and boots. In the golden light of the Antarctic morning, we melted lumps of ice in a pan over the stove. We drank some of the hot water and used the rest to make instant oatmeal for breakfast.

One by one, the people around the camp woke up and emerged from their snow shelters. In a few hours,

The late-night sun hangs over the southern tip of Ross Island (right), the point where the permanent ice shelf begins. It takes a while to get used to the fact that the sun never sets during the summer season.

Survival school participants check for crevasses as they cross a glacier (right) *and use ice axes to climb a steep hillside* (below).

we were on our way over to the steep slopes of Ross Island, where we spent the morning learning how to cross snowfields and glaciers. Patient instructors demonstrated how to use an ice ax to probe the snow for hidden crevasses or holes and how to cut steps in sheer icy cliffs. They also showed us how to use the ice ax as a brake in case we slipped and started sliding downhill.

After a rest and a power lunch of nuts, raisins, candy, and water, the day ended with a hike up to a high outcropping of rock called Castle Rock. It was a long walk in heavy gear, but the view from the top was spectacular. Massive glaciers ran down from the island and formed great cliffs of ice where they met the frozen sea. Mount Erebus towered in the distance, its peak hidden in clouds. To the south, the ice shelf stretched to the horizon, an unbroken sheet of white.

After spending three days in the ice and snow, I was much more prepared for the unexpected. I had learned the skills I needed to survive, and I had practiced everything firsthand. Now I felt ready to join the Antarctic researchers who work in this harsh environment.

One afternoon during survival school, we hiked to Castle Rock.

A young Weddell seal lies out on the sea ice, watching me. Of all Antarctic seal species, Weddell seals live the farthest south and in the most inhospitable environment.

Chapter 4

Weddell Seals

Two Weddell seals surface for air.

Early one gray, overcast morning, I left McMurdo with Lori Williams, one of the science support staff at the station, in a small, tracked vehicle called a Spryte. Lori was driving and showing me how to steer. Sprytes don't have a steering wheel, just two rods mounted on the floor in front of the driver's seat: one to control the vehicle's left track and one to control the right.

We were heading north along one of the flagged routes toward Big Razorback Island, about 15 miles from Mc-Murdo. Near the base of the island, Dr. J. Ward Testa from the University of Alaska at Fairbanks had a field camp on the sea ice. A veteran Antarctic researcher, Dr. Testa was studying seals that live around McMurdo Sound.

The windchill was -58° F. Even with the heater running full blast, it was very cold in the Spryte, and frost kept building up on the windshield. Despite the frost and the dark clouds that hung low over the sound, Big Razorback Island was easy to see from a distance—a dark jagged mass rising up from the ice. As we got closer to the island, we could also see the orange research hut of the field camp.

From this sea ice field camp, Dr. Ward Testa's research team studies the Weddell seal population in McMurdo Sound.

When we arrived, Ward was sitting at a table in the center of the one-room hut, entering data into a laptop computer. He welcomed us in and introduced Jason Schreer, one of the graduate students working with him. Lori and I took off our boots and parkas and huddled around the hut's large heater. Next to the heater was a wall of shelves heaped with cans and boxes of food. At the far end of the room were two sets of bunk beds and more shelves. Near the door, a cooking area had been set up with a Coleman stove, a sink, water containers, and stacks of pots and pans.

For more than 10 years, Ward Testa had been coming down to Antarctica every spring to study Weddell seals.

He was investigating how the seal population in the sound changes from year to year. Part of his research involved trying to identify the factors that affect the number of seal pups produced each year and the survival rates of both pups and adults. He was also interested in tracking the seals during the winter and studying their behavior under water.

Truly at home in the sea, a Weddell seal cruises along under the sea ice.

In addition to Weddell seals, three other species of seals make Antarctica their home. Ross, crabeater, and leopard seals live along the outer edges of the pack ice, near the open sea. Weddell seals, on the other hand, live close to land, where thick ice covers the sea's surface for more than eight months of the year. During that time, Weddell seals' only access to air is through breathing holes in the ice.

One big advantage for Weddell seals in living under the sea ice is safety from predators—leopard seals and killer whales stay near open water and will not swim long distances under the ice.

Ward was anxious to get on with his work for the day, so after a cup of hot tea we got ready to go. Our first task was to try to locate several seals that were wearing satellite-linked time/depth recorders, called "satpaks" for short.

Satpaks had been attached to about a dozen female seals the year before. Now that the seals had returned to their breeding sites after the long winter, Ward and Jason were trying to retrieve as many of the satpaks as

In winter, Weddell seals spend nearly all of their time in the water. During those long, dark months, it is much colder out of the water than in it. In the spring, however, adult seals come up onto the sea ice near land and form breeding colonies. By mid-October, breeding colonies of Weddell seals dot the sea ice all around the edges of McMurdo Sound and its islands.

Members of a Weddell seal colony—mostly mothers and pups—stretch out on the ice.

possible. The data they contained could tell the scientists a great deal about what Weddell seals do in the wintertime.

We loaded a good-sized antenna, several ice axes, and all the necessary survival gear into the back of the Spryte and drove off across the ice. Ward and Jason were very familiar with the ice in this area, so they knew what spots to avoid. It didn't take long to reach nearby Tent Island, a small volcanic peak that was farther out in the sound. There were pressure ridges along the shoreline where the sea ice had been pushed up against the land with great force, causing it to buckle and heave. Ward parked the Spryte out on flat, safe ice, and we crossed the pressure ridges on foot, using ice axes to test for weak spots before taking each step. The ice was riddled with cracks that were hidden under thin crusts of snow.

The island's steep hillsides were covered with loose, gravelly volcanic rock, and it took nearly 20 minutes to scramble up to a high ridge that overlooked McMurdo Sound. But we couldn't stand up because of the wind, which was strong enough to sweep a person right off the ridge. We had to work on our hands and knees.

Ward set up a receiver on the ground and put on earphones. Then hoisting the antenna as high as possible, he waited, straining to hear over the roar of the wind. If any seals wearing satpaks were in the area, Ward should have been able to pick up the satpak signals with this equipment. But after a few minutes he shook his head, and shouted, "Nothing. The seals must not be within range. We'll try again tomorrow. Let's go down before we all get frostbitten."

With hoods up to protect our faces, we hurried back down to the Spryte and drove toward the first of several seal colonies that were near Big Razorback Island. I could see seals from a long way off—they looked like dark blobs scattered here and there on the ice.

Satpaks record information about the length and depth of the seals' dives. They also send out a signal that is picked up by satellites orbiting the earth. The satellites pinpoint the exact location of the signal's source, and then transmit this information back to earth. In this way, researchers are able to follow the movements of the seals in places where they themselves cannot go—for example, under the sea ice during the Antarctic winter.

Many years ago, researchers began tagging the Weddell seals that live in McMurdo Sound in order to keep track of individuals from year to year. These seals have become some of the most well-studied seals in Antarctica. As a result of this tagging program, scientists have discovered that female Weddells often return again and again to the same breeding sites to give birth to their pups.

The identification tags on this seal are clearly visible on the rear flippers.

Ward stopped the Spryte some distance from the colony, and we quietly approached the animals that were stretched out on the ice. Most of the seals appeared to be sleeping. Some were even snoring. Those that were awake paid little attention to us. One of the remarkable things about most of Antarctica's animals is that it's possible to get very close to them—they have little fear of humans. Weddell seals' natural enemies—killer whales and leopard seals—are in the water, so they feel safe on top of the ice.

There were 15 adult seals here, and nearly all of them were females with pups. Weddell seals give birth near the end of October, so this was the height of the pupping season. The mother seals were all very fat and sleek, with glossy gray-black fur spotted with light gray. The pups had fluffy brown or gray fur. Most of the pups looked like they were only a few days old.

Ward and Jason slowly walked up to the nearest female. She was sleeping on her side, her sausage-shaped body stretched out full-length on the ice. From her nose to her flippers, she was about 10 feet long and probably weighed around 1,000 pounds. A fluffy brown pup lay next to her on the snow, dwarfed by its huge mother. The female opened her eyes and lazily rolled over onto her stomach. As she spread her flippers, I could see brightly colored identification tags attached to them.

Each season, Ward and his assistants tackle the major task of recording the tag numbers of all the adult seals they come across and tagging all the newborn pups. The Antarctic Treaty prohibits close contact with the continent's wildlife, except for specific scientific purposes. Ward and Jason had special permits that allowed them to touch and tag the seals. I didn't, so I could only stand and watch.

Weddell seals may not be afraid of people, but like all mothers, the females are protective of their young. It

Ward Testa attaches a tag to the rear flipper of a newborn pup (left). The red strand on the pup's belly is a frozen bit of its umbilical cord. This pup hardly seemed to mind being tagged, and its mother paid almost no attention to the scientists.

Jason needed to distract this pup's mother while Ward tagged the pup.

was Jason's job to distract each mother seal so that Ward could tag her pup. Jason slowly approached this female, waving a bear paw mitt in front of her face to attract her attention. She eyed the mitt for a moment. Then, with a harsh, growling sort of bark, she snapped at it. Jason took a big step backward. The mother seal followed, humping her huge body across the ice.

Now Ward had his chance. He quickly knelt down next to the pup and checked whether it was a male or female. Then, using a pair of what looked like large pliers, he attached a green plastic numbered tag to the pup's right rear flipper. The pup let out a loud ''baaahhh'' and tried to wriggle away. Hearing her baby's cry, the mother seal spun around and humped back toward the pup. But by then Ward was finished and had moved off to a safe distance. Using a hand-held computer, he recorded the sex and tag number of the pup and the tag number of its mother.

In the meantime, the mother seal sniffed and nuzzled her pup, making sure it was all right. The pup snuggled up to its mother and looked back at us with huge

A mother Weddell seal and her pup lie out on the sea ice, soaking up the pale spring sunshine.

An adult Weddell seal has a layer of blubber about four inches thick just under its skin. That thick layer of fat is excellent insulation—it locks the seal's body heat inside. On a calm, sunny day, adult Weddell seals can actually get too warm out on the ice and must take a plunge in the icy sea to cool off.

brown eyes. When Ward was confident that both mother and baby were behaving normally, we moved on.

The next female was much more aggressive. With jaws snapping, she bellowed and lunged again and again at Jason. The pup, on the other hand, hardly seemed bothered by what was going on.

Ward and Jason moved from one pair to the next in the colony. Each time they found a newborn pup, they tagged it. They also recorded the tag numbers of all the tagged adults in the colony. The two men worked as quickly as possible. They wanted to keep their contact with the seals to a minimum—and it was really cold! Standing out on the ice, exposed to the bitter wind, we humans were getting chilled to the bone, but the seals around us were perfectly comfortable.

Our path through the colony took us close to some huge pressure ridges. In this area of heaved-up blocks of ice, there were breathing holes and cracks where the seals got in and out of the water. Most of the holes were hidden among the ridges of ice. We could hear the gasping sputters of seals in the water coming up for air, but couldn't see them.

Finally we found a hole out in the open. While I watched, a whiskered head appeared above the dark water. The seal took a long look around, its large nostrils opening and closing with each breath. Then it dropped a few inches below the surface, opened its mouth, and began to thrash its head from side to side— it was clearing away newly formed ice from the edge of the hole. Like all other marine mammals, Weddell seals need to come to the surface to breathe air. But their breathing holes freeze over very quickly. To keep these vital openings clear, the seals have specialized front teeth that flare out at an angle, and they can open their jaws very wide. Using their teeth as grinding tools, the seals gnaw away any ice that builds up around the edges of their breathing holes.

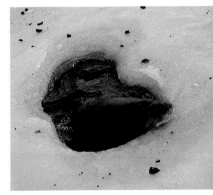

Using specialized front teeth, a Weddell seal enlarges its breathing hole (above) *and another chews through thin ice covering open water* (below).

On top of the ice, Weddell seals seem clumsy and awkward as they hump around like giant overweight caterpillars. But in the water, they are agile and quick, able to roll, turn, and spin with seemingly weightless ease. They are also remarkable divers. When hunting for a meal of fish or squid, Weddell seals often dive as deep as two thousand feet beneath the ice and may stay underwater for nearly an hour before coming up for air. They can do this because they are able to store large amounts of oxygen in their blood and muscles—more than 13 times the amount they can carry in one lungful of air. This adaptation makes it possible for Weddell seals to dive deep and to swim long distances under the ice before having to come up for air.

When all the pups in this colony had been tagged, we drove over to a larger colony about half a mile away. There were 20 females at this site, and again most of them had pups. This was a windy spot for a nursery, and some of the pups were almost completely covered with snow.

Ward and Jason methodically worked their way through the pairs of mothers and pups. Some of the pups in this colony were older and bigger and had already been tagged. Weddell seal pups grow very quickly, drinking their mother's rich milk—it has about 20 times more fat than cow's milk. In a few more days, these larger pups would be big enough to accompany their mothers into the sea.

By the end of the afternoon, after visiting three more seal colonies, the day's tagging work was done. During the next two months, Ward and his field assistants would visit all the seal colonies in the area many times. By mid-November, the pupping season would be over, and all of the pups would be tagged. But even then the researchers would continue their tag-reading program in order to keep track of which seals were where on the ice. They'd log between five thousand and ten thousand individual seal tag readings into their computer before the research season was over. All the data about the McMurdo Sound seals would be added to the growing body of information that has been gathered over many years about Weddell seals in Antarctica.

In his research, Ward Testa has discovered some interesting facts about how the McMurdo Sound seal population changes from year to year. About every fourth or fifth year, fewer than the normal number of pups are born. During these same years, fewer adult seals survive the winter. As a result, the seal population temporarily decreases. There are fewer seals for a year or so, but then the population returns to its normal size.

What might cause such a cycle? Weddell seals are near the top of the Antarctic food web. Decreases in the numbers of new pups born and the adult survival rate are most likely a result of a decrease in the seals' food supply. But what could affect the numbers of fish that swim in the ocean around Antarctica every four or five years?

Ward has speculated that there may be a link between the population fluctuations of Weddell seals and something called El Niño. El Niño is a peculiar warming of the Pacific Ocean near the equator that takes place roughly every four years. During the years when El Niño occurs, weather patterns are disrupted all over the world. Ocean circulation patterns change, too. Ward has suggested that in years when changes in ocean circulation are brought about by El Niño, fewer fish wind up in Antarctic waters. With less food available, female Weddell seals are less likely to have pups, and fewer adult seals survive. When El Niño is over, ocean circulation patterns—and the fish supply—return to normal, and the seal population recovers. It's an interesting hypothesis.

When Lori and I left the seal camp that night, the clouds were gone and the sun was casting a golden glow over the frozen surface of the sound. As we drove along, I couldn't help wondering how many seals were beneath us right then, swimming and diving in the shadowy world under the ice.

Marvelously well-adapted to a frozen world, a Weddell seal rests on the sea ice.

Bryan Johnson holds tight to a helium-filled balloon, which will carry an ozone-measuring instrument into the ozone layer over McMurdo.

Chapter 5

The Hole in the Sky

"Now just hold on tight right here while I tie off the bottom of the balloon," Bryan Johnson said. "It's going to pull a bit, so hang on."

Bryan and I were kneeling on a heavy canvas tarp spread out on the stony ground. Above our heads, a helium-filled balloon made of thin, nearly transparent plastic swayed and bobbed in the wind. I kept a tight grip on it while Bryan slipped off his mittens and carefully tied a knot in the plastic at the bottom. Above the knot he secured a cord that was attached to a duct tape-wrapped package about the size of a toaster. Inside the package was an instrument called an ozonesonde, which would measure the amount of ozone gas in the surrounding air.

I watched Bryan's fingers turn white as he tightly knotted the cord again and again. It was a Condition 2 day—gray, windy, and bitterly cold. We were working beside a tall building at the edge of McMurdo, overlooking the sound. The building blocked the wind somewhat. But out in the sound, the wind was just roaring along, sending clouds of snow swirling across the sea ice.

Richard Thompson returned from putting away the hose we'd used to fill the balloon with helium. He reached up to steady the balloon as Bryan finished tying on the ozonesonde. Now it was just a matter of waiting for a break in the wind so that we could launch it.

Richard walked down to the edge of a metal platform that jutted out from the hillside. He turned his face into the wind, feeling its strength, waiting for a moment of calm. Crouching low, Bryan and I carried the balloon a few yards away from the building, toward a more open spot. Gusts of wind tugged at the thin plastic. If

Bryan (left) gets a hand inflating an ozonesonde-carrying balloon from fellow ozone researchers Louise Emmons and Lori Perliski.

During a brief lull in the wind, the balloon is launched.

we let go now, it would be blown down against the ground and ripped to shreds. We kept our eyes on Richard and waited.

The wind kept gusting for several more minutes. Then, quite suddenly, it died down. "OK, let it go!" shouted Richard, waving his arms in case we couldn't hear him. I stepped back as Bryan took a few steps forward, raised the balloon above his head, and released it.

Most of the world's ozone is found in a distinct layer in the stratosphere, the region of the atmosphere that is roughly between 6.5 and 30 miles above the earth's surface. Without the ozone layer, our planet's surface would be bombarded by ultraviolet (UV) rays that are powerful enough to kill some living things and damage most others. But in the ozone layer, ozone molecules—made up of three oxygen atoms—absorb high-energy UV rays coming from the sun and prevent them from reaching the earth.

The timing was perfect. The wind returned with a savage gust, but it didn't matter any more. The balloon was safely sailing upward into the steely gray sky, billowing and twisting like it was alive. It grew smaller and smaller until it disappeared into the clouds.

"Come on, you can watch the data coming in," Bryan urged. We hurried inside the building and climbed a narrow spiral staircase that led to a dome-shaped room at the very top. At one end of the room, a laptop computer and several pieces of electronic equipment were set up on a makeshift table.

"It's working great," said Richard. Numbers flashed across the computer screen—data coming back to earth from the ozonesonde as it traveled skyward. It was continually transmitting information about the amount of ozone in the air around it. This data would keep coming in until the balloon reached a height of about 22 miles, at which point it would burst and the ozonesonde would fall back to earth.

The numbers flashing across the computer screen didn't mean much to me at first. But later on, when the data had been plotted on a graph, I could see that on this day in mid-October, there was far less than the normal amount of ozone in the atmosphere above us. We were under the Antarctic ozone hole.

Beginning in late August each year, a drastic thinning of the ozone layer takes place over Antarctica as huge amounts of ozone disappear from the stratosphere above the continent. This "hole" in the ozone layer lasts until November, when ozone levels gradually return to normal. Antarctic scientists first noticed this seasonal ozone hole in the late 1970s. It quickly became the focus of an international research effort. Today scientists know a great deal about Antarctica's ozone hole. They also know that stratospheric ozone destruction has become a worldwide environmental problem.

Bryan Johnson and Richard Thompson were part of a team of ozone researchers from the University of Wyoming. They had arrived in McMurdo at the end of August, on the first flight in for the season. Weather permitting, they had been launching ozonesondes nearly every day since then. Each set of readings they received from an ozonesonde added to the picture of what was happening in the ozone layer above the continent.

While Bryan and Richard were launching ozonesondes, other teams of researchers were using different instruments to study the ozone hole. One afternoon, Lori Perliski from the National Oceanographic and Atmospheric Administration in Boulder, Colorado, and Louise Emmons from the University of New York at Stony Brook drove me up to a small research hut in the hills above McMurdo. There they showed me the Dobson spectrophotometers they were using to study the chemical makeup of the stratosphere overhead. A Dobson spectrophotometer is a ground-based instrument that

The main culprits in the ozone destruction story are chlorofluorocarbons (CFCs). These manufactured chemicals, which easily evaporate into the air, were widely used as coolants in refrigerators and air conditioners, as propellants in aerosol sprays, and in the manufacturing process for all sorts of foam products. Millions of tons of CFCs have been released into the atmosphere since people began using them in the 1930s. And even though CFCs are safe, nontoxic, nonreactive compounds down on earth, once they reach the stratosphere, UV rays break them apart to release ozone-destroying chlorine atoms.

New Zealand scientist Sylvia Nichol was also using Dobson spectrophotometers to study ozone destruction above Antarctica. She had set one up outside on the snow. It was wrapped in a thick insulating cover to protect it from the intense cold.

Each year, around the end of April, the sun slips below the horizon over Antarctica and isn't seen again until the end of August. Its disappearance marks the beginning of about four months of winter darkness when it gets extremely cold, both on land and in the atmosphere above the continent.

In the stratosphere, high-altitude winds form an enormous ring of moving air, called the Antarctic polar vortex. As winter progresses, the air inside the vortex eventually gets so cold that rare polar stratospheric clouds form.

Throughout the winter, the icy particles that make up polar stratospheric clouds combine and interact with various molecules and atoms in the stratosphere, particularly those that have been released during the breakdown of CFCs. When the first rays of spring sunlight strike the icy chemical mix in the polar vortex, they trigger a series of reactions in which billions of chlorine atoms are released. This leads to massive ozone destruction above the continent. In short, a "hole" forms in the ozone layer.

Antarctic polar stratospheric clouds are best seen when the sun is just below the horizon.

measures the amounts of ozone and some types of ozone-destroying molecules in the stratosphere.

Other McMurdo scientists were using laser beams to study polar stratospheric clouds, which play a key role in the ozone hole's formation. With an instrument called a lidar (short for light radar), they directed pulses of powerful green laser light up into the stratosphere. Some of the light beams struck the icy particles making up the clouds and bounced back. By measuring various characteristics of the returning light, these researchers could tell a lot about the clouds' composition, size, and altitude.

Scientists also use instruments aboard satellites orbiting the earth to study the ozone hole. Satellite-borne Total Ozone Mapping Spectrometers (TOMS) monitor the status of the ozone layer all over the world. They send back images from space that give researchers a broad view of ozone destruction and show how the Antarctic ozone hole changes from day to day.

When researchers bring together information from ground-based instruments, ozonesondes, and satellites, a fairly accurate picture of what is happening in the ozone

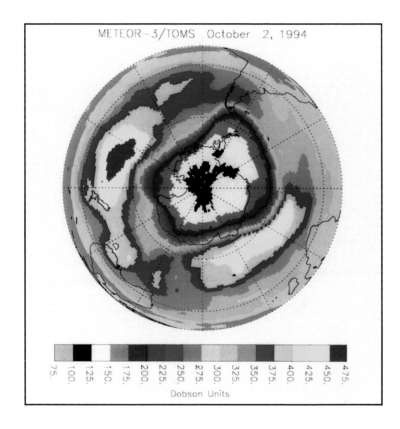

METEOR-3/TOMS   October   2, 1994

75. 100. 125. 150. 175. 200. 225. 250. 275. 300. 325. 350. 375. 400. 425. 450. 475.

Dobson Units

This TOMS image shows ozone destruction over Antarctica on October 2, 1994. The area of greatest ozone loss is shown in black.

layer above Antarctica emerges. Each spring two-thirds of the total amount of ozone over the continent is destroyed. At certain altitudes, all of the ozone disappears. And the problem seems to be getting worse. Each year's hole develops earlier, lasts longer, and is deeper—more ozone is destroyed—than the previous year's hole.

The ozone layer absorbs the types of ultraviolet (UV) rays that are most damaging to living things. Less ozone in the stratosphere means that more harmful UV radiation is reaching the planet's surface. Each spring, as huge amounts of ozone disappear over Antarctica, harmful UV radiation strikes the continent and the sea around it. What effects are those UV rays having on life at the bottom of the world?

In early spring and summer, portable fish huts (above) dot the sea ice on McMurdo Sound. Some are positioned over holes in the ice (below) to serve as shelters for researchers who are collecting phytoplankton or other marine organisms.

Fish Hut #9 sat out on the sea ice in the middle of McMurdo Sound, at the end of one of the flagged routes. It was a squat little building with a square trapdoor in the floor. The opening was positioned directly over a perfectly shaped circular hole that had been cut into the sea ice. A soft, turquoise blue light lit up the sides of the hole. The water in the center was inky black.

"The ice is about two meters thick out here, maybe a little more," said Dr. Michael Lesser, as he propped the trapdoor up against the wall. "If you look closely, you can see that the underside of the ice has a kind of brownish, greenish cast. That's phytoplankton."

Michael was from the Bigelow Laboratory in Maine. He was showing me how to collect phytoplankton from McMurdo Sound. These phytoplankton were being used in several UV radiation experiments. Michael and his colleague Dr. Patrick Neale from the University of California at Berkeley had come to McMurdo to find out if these tiny marine organisms were being affected—

even under the ice—by the UV rays that were coming through the Antarctic ozone hole.

"We drop a plankton net down into the water," Michael explained, "and then swirl it around a bit, so that it scrapes against the underside of the ice. When it comes up, it's full of tiny bits of ice and lots of phytoplankton."

Outside the hut, the scientists had set up an experimental chamber out on the ice. The bottom half looked

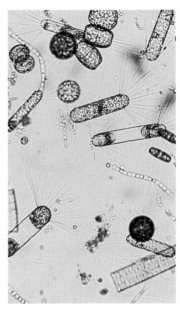

Phytoplankton are single-celled photosynthetic organisms that drift through the oceans. Most are too small to be seen without a microscope. In spring, the underside of the sea ice is thick with phytoplankton, especially the types known as diatoms.

Dr. Michael Lesser collects a sample of phytoplankton from one compartment of the experimental chamber set up on the sea ice outside Fish Hut #9.

Phytoplankton form the base of the Antarctic food web. Many small marine animals eat plankton, and they, in turn, are eaten by other animals like penguins and seals. All the animals that live in Antarctic waters ultimately depend on phytoplankton. Scientists are concerned that the increased amounts of harmful UV rays that now bombard Antarctica each spring may eventually have a negative effect on phytoplankton in the seas around the continent. And whatever affects the phytoplankton will sooner or later affect the rest of the Antarctic food web.

like a bright orange, rectangular box about the size of a small table. On top of this were two compartments, each filled with seawater and some of the phytoplankton that Michael and the others had collected. Heating coils ran underneath both compartments, keeping the water inside between 28° F and 29° F, the same temperature as the seawater under the ice.

The two compartments were exactly the same, except for their lids. The lid of one compartment was made out of a type of Plexiglas that blocked UV rays. The other lid was made out of Plexiglas that UV rays could pass right through. A fine black mesh covered both compartments. This helped to duplicate the lighting conditions that exist in the sea under two meters of ice.

Every few days, a member of the research team would drive out here in a Spryte and collect samples of phytoplankton from each compartment. Back in McMurdo, the samples were analyzed to see how well the phytoplankton were photosynthesizing and growing.

The results were very interesting. The phytoplankton that were exposed to UV rays didn't photosynthesize as much or grow as well as the phytoplankton kept on the protected side. Researchers in other parts of Antarctica were getting similar results in other types of experiments on plankton. It seems that even under the ice, the higher-than-normal amounts of harmful UV rays coming through the ozone hole can damage phytoplankton and other small forms of marine life.

Michael slipped on a pair of plastic surgical gloves and collected new plankton samples from each compartment to take back to the lab. After the lids were back on and everything was securely fastened down against the wind, we went back to the fish hut to warm up and replace the trapdoor over the hole in the ice. As we were covering the hole, we caught sight of a seal in the water just below us. Moments later it surfaced and exhaled with a loud snort, blowing warm, fishy breath in our faces. The seal looked around with large brown eyes, and then dove back down into the depths.

"We know that the increased amount of UV is affecting the plankton," Michael said, after the seal had disappeared. "But no one knows if it's having any direct effect on seals or penguins. Some people have suggested that it might damage their eyes, but at this point, that's just a guess."

Most of the ozone studies and UV experiments are concluded in early November, as the amount of ozone in the stratosphere over Antarctica gradually returns to normal levels. Most of the scientists who flew down to study the ozone hole then head home, where they begin analyzing the data they collected that season. But a few scientists keep right on traveling north. At research stations in the Arctic, they use ozonesondes, Dobson spectrophotometers, and other instruments to measure the stratospheric ozone loss that now takes place at the top of the world each spring. So far, it hasn't been enough to cause an ozone hole over the North Pole. But the amount of ozone that is destroyed each spring is greater every year. That's not a good sign. Neither is the fact that the total amount of stratospheric ozone worldwide is gradually decreasing. This global loss isn't a seasonal variation, like an ozone hole, but a steady, continuing decline. It means that earth's protective ozone shield is getting thinner everywhere.

The good news is that ozone depletion is an environmental problem that can be solved. Once people stop producing and using CFCs, along with several other ozone-destroying chemicals, the ozone layer will eventually recover and return to normal. But as long as there is an ozone hole over Antarctica each spring, teams of ozone researchers will be there to study it.

The bodies of Antarctic birds and mammals are well protected from ultraviolet (UV) radiation by fur and feathers. But their eyes may be sensitive to damage by higher-than-normal amounts of harmful UV rays coming through the ozone hole.

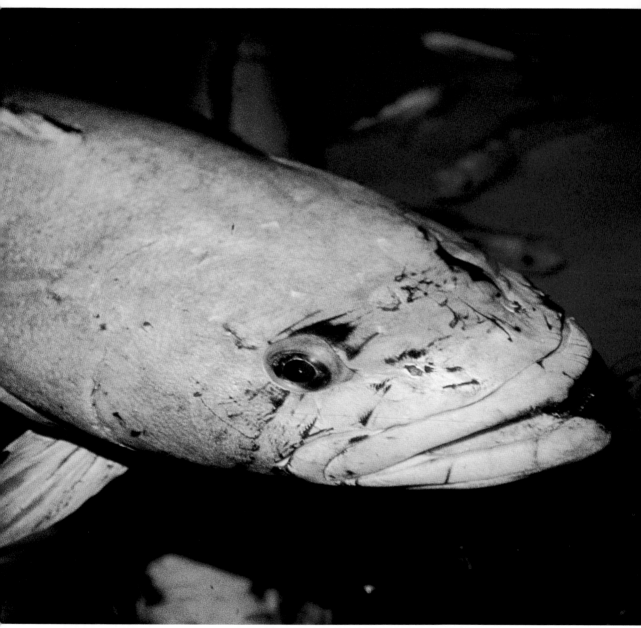

Antarctic fish live in an environment where the water around them is always on the brink of freezing. Natural antifreeze proteins in their blood keep them from freezing in this icy world.

Chapter 6
Going Fishing

If you put an ordinary fish like a trout or a tuna into McMurdo Sound, it would freeze to death in less than a minute. The temperature of Antarctic waters hovers around 28° F, the freezing point of seawater. Yet some species of fish thrive in icy polar seas. Why don't *they* freeze?

For more than 30 years, scientists working in Mc-Murdo have been looking for answers to that question. Dr. Art DeVries, an American researcher from the University of Illinois, pioneered the study of Antarctic fishes and their remarkable ability to survive in such cold water. He discovered that fishes living in the sea around Antarctica have antifreeze in their blood. Not the kind of antifreeze that people put into cars, but a natural antifreeze made up of special proteins called glycoproteins.

My experience with scientists who study fish antifreeze proteins began one night in the galley when I met three people who were part of Art DeVries's research team. Hans Ramløv was a Danish cryobiologist. Cryobiologists study the effects of extremely low temperatures on living things. He and Lisa Karnick, a German biologist, and Richard Willis, a New Zealand researcher, were all

Fresh water freezes at 32° Fahrenheit, or 0° Celsius. Seawater has a lower freezing point mainly because of all the salt it contains.

Antifreeze proteins do two things that make it possible for Antarctic fishes to survive in 28°F waters. The proteins lower the freezing point of the fishes' blood, and they keep both blood and body fluids from freezing by blocking the formation of ice crystals. Whenever crystals of ice start to form inside a fish's body, antifreeze proteins bind to the crystals and stop them from growing any larger.

going to spend the season studying antifreeze proteins in a very large species of fish called Antarctic cod. But before they could study these fish, they had to catch some. They invited me to come along and see how it was done.

Early the next morning, we left McMurdo in a pick-up-style Spryte. It was a still, heavily overcast day—I could feel a change coming in the weather. Once out of McMurdo, Hans drove along a flagged route that led across the sea ice toward the middle of the sound. The flags ended abruptly at Fish Hut #4, about four miles from the station.

The hut was much like others I had visited, a small wooden shed with a single window, a heater in one corner, and a square opening in the floor positioned over a hole in the ice. There was something different here, though: a large, motorized winch had been bolted to the floor next to the hole, and from it a metal cable ran down into the sea.

A sheet of plywood had been laid over the hole to help keep the open water from freezing solid. But tiny fragments of slushy ice had formed on the surface, so we had to clear this away before doing anything else. Using nets attached to long poles, we scooped up the slush and tossed it outside the open door. This cleared the ice out of the hole, but it made for a very tricky first step in or out of the hut!

With the slushy ice gone, the circular pool of sea water in the hole was as clear as glass. While I watched, a huge Weddell seal suddenly surfaced. "Hello, Aurora!" called Lisa, with a grin. "She's a regular visitor, our Aurora. She comes up whenever we start making noise in here."

Aurora was a beautiful seal. Her sleek coat was mottled with silvery gray spots that shimmered in the light. She made no sound, but simply bobbed gently up and

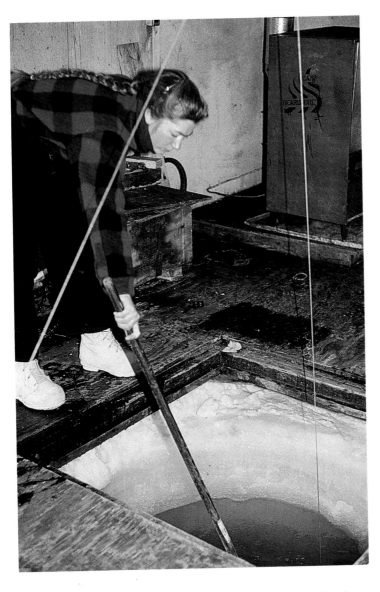

Using a pole net, German biologist Lisa Karnick clears the slushy ice from a hole in the sea ice.

Aurora, a big Weddell seal, visits Fish Hut #4. The fishing line for catching Antarctic cod is in front of her.

down in the hole and watched us. "This could take a while," Richard said. "I think Aurora enjoys watching us, and she's been known to hang around for a long time. She actually fell asleep in the hole once."

These scientists had special permits that allowed them

to catch a few cod for their research. But there was nothing we could do to encourage the seal to leave and let us get on with our work. We just had to wait for her to leave on her own. So as the minutes ticked by, Aurora watched us, and we watched her. It was quite wonderful to be so close to such a huge animal. Eventually, though, she seemed to tire of us, and with a kick of her flippers, she was gone.

Richard started up the winch, and the cable began slowly winding up. He then sat down in an old, battered easy chair nearby and stretched out his legs. "Well, we might as well be comfortable while we wait," he explained. "That line is 750 meters long and it'll take about 20 minutes to bring it up."

Time passed quickly because Aurora hadn't finished with us yet. She popped up into the hole every few minutes, perhaps to see if there had been any interesting developments. Just after Aurora's third visit, Lisa caught a glimpse of something shiny in the water below. There was a pale shape suspended in the blackness, coming closer and closer. It was a fish on the line.

And what a fish! As Hans stopped the winch, Richard stepped down onto a small metal platform that hung over one side of the hole and grabbed hold of the gills of an Antarctic cod that was almost as large as he was. The fish thrashed back and forth, sending icy water everywhere. Hans and Lisa took hold of Richard and together the three of them heaved the struggling fish clear of the hole.

Working quickly, they laid the fish down in a long V-shaped wooden tray, and then measured and weighed it. Finally the researchers eased the fish into a long, narrow, metal-lined box full of seawater. It was a tight fit; the fish's tail had to be tucked in.

We all helped bolt the lid to the box while Lisa attached an air pump with a hose that ran into a hole in

Richard Willis gets a grip on a giant Antarctic cod. This is the safest way, for both cod and human, to lift what turned out to be a 64-inch-long and 88-pound fish.

the lid so that the fish could get the oxygen it needed during the trip back to McMurdo. Struggling to keep our balance, we carried the box through the icy doorway and hoisted it up onto the back of the Spryte. Richard baited the line again and ran it back down into the deep water. After covering the hole and closing up the hut, we were ready to go.

Lisa eases the huge fish into a specially designed box for the trip back to McMurdo.

Hans and Lisa load the fish into the back of the Spryte.

Riding in the back of a pickup-style Spryte is a good way to get chilled to the bone.

It was important to get the fish back to the aquarium in McMurdo as fast as possible. But while we had been working inside the hut, the weather had changed. It had started snowing, and the wind had picked up. Great clouds of blowing snow were sweeping along the sea ice. We couldn't see Ross Island. There was just bright, flat whiteness in every direction.

Hans and I got into the cab of the Spryte, while Richard and Lisa climbed up onto the open back. They had the unpleasant job of sitting on top of the fish's box in order to keep it from sliding and bumping as the vehicle traveled over the rough ice and snow. While Hans drove, I watched for flags. The flagged route had seemed ridiculously easy to follow before. But now when we passed a flag, I could just barely make out the next one in line ahead of us.

Back with the fish, Richard and Lisa were having a hard time. Blowing snow quickly covered them. Their breath froze into the neck gaiters covering their faces, turning the fabric into a rock-hard mask of ice.

Once Hans made a wrong turn at a point where several flagged routes intersected. Precious minutes ticked by as we had to retrace our path to get back on the right route. Every now and then, the wind died down, and like a veil being lifted, the air would clear enough to reveal Ross Island faintly in the distance. It took nearly 45 minutes to cross the sea ice and reach the station.

After checking back in with Mac Center, Hans drove along the shoreline to the old aquarium building. We all worked together to carry the box inside, past rows of small glass aquariums and a half dozen circular holding tanks where the Antarctic cod were kept. The place smelled of fish and saltwater.

We set the box down in an open space and took off

The three researchers lift the new arrival into a tank at the aquarium building in McMurdo.

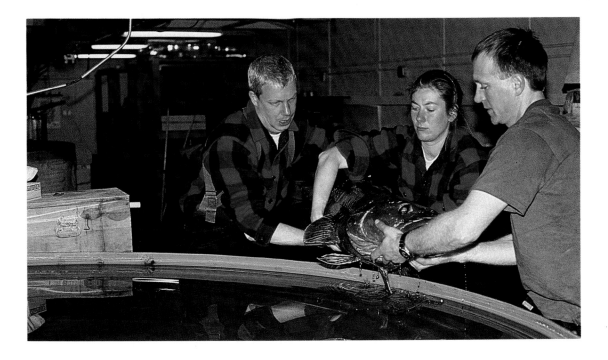

the lid. The occupant was very still and pale. With Richard at the head, Lisa in the middle, and Hans taking the tail, the three researchers gently lifted the fish into the nearest holding tank.

There was one cod already in this tank, a big hulk nicknamed Alex. He cruised slowly around the tank, his bulging eyes taking in the newcomer as well as the scientists all leaning over his watery domain. Compared to Alex, the new fish was very pale and rather listless—

Hans Ramløv pulls the newly caught cod back and forth in the tank to get water circulating around its gills. This is a quick way to get more oxygen to the fish. The sign on the wall reads: "Experiment in Progress. Do Not Feed, Pinch, Fondle, or Kiss the Fish."

probably in shock from being caught and then kept in the box so long during the slow drive back. With both hands on its tail, Hans gently moved the new fish back and forth so that the water washed over its gills. After a few minutes of this treatment, the fish perked up and started to swim slowly around the tank.

Alex didn't pay much attention to his new tankmate. He seemed much more interested in the fingers that strayed into the water now and then as we worked. "Gotta be careful around these fish," Richard said. "Look at the size of their mouths—they can easily bite your hand off."

With the fish we had caught that morning, there were seven Antarctic cod here in the tanks, ready for the studies on antifreeze proteins to begin. Over the next few months, blood and tissue samples would be taken from these fish and others that would be caught later in the season. After extracting glycoproteins from the samples, researchers would conduct experiments in which they would study how the proteins prevent ice crystals from growing and forming sharp edges.

If scientists ever isolate the fish gene that codes for antifreeze proteins, it may be possible to produce the proteins synthetically in the laboratory. Perhaps the ice cream you eat one day will contain natural antifreeze proteins that will prevent hard ice crystals from forming and ruining its creamy texture—the same proteins that protect Antarctic fish from freezing in icy polar seas.

Two Antarctic cod circle each other in a tank.

An Antarctic sea star feeds on a bush sponge.

Chapter 7
Under the Ice

One clear, cold Sunday morning I got a ride over to New Zealand's Scott Base, which is only a couple of miles from McMurdo. I was let off at the edge of a gravelly road, not far from the station's half dozen light-green buildings that are clustered by the shore. Beyond the buildings, massive pressure ridges ran along the shoreline. The great, upheaved blocks of ice were tinted in shades of pale blue, turquoise, and green. A lone Weddell seal was taking a snooze near the bottom of one, soaking up the sun.

On my way up to the main building, I waved to a few Scott Base residents who were working outside. They were bundled up in the New Zealand version of polar survival gear: bright yellow parkas and coveralls. A flight of steps led up to the station's main entrance where, just inside the airlock, a sign reminded visitors that there were "no boots allowed" beyond that point. I left my boots and parka by the door, and padded inside in stocking feet.

Dr. Chris Battershill was waiting for me as I came in. "Good morning," he said. "How about a cup of tea?" He took me into the station's cozy galley, where we sat

Delicate sea urchins are common on the Antarctic seafloor.

73

Most of the buildings at Scott Base are connected and elevated above ground, so blowing snow won't bury them in drifts. Offshore, massive pressure ridges border the land.

and drank tea and talked about his research. As a marine ecologist with the New Zealand Oceanographic Institute, Chris was in Antarctica studying the communities of plants and animals that live on the seafloor near the island. Many of these benthic organisms, as such bottom-dwellers are called, are unique to this continent. To carry out his research, Chris and his colleagues were doing what only a handful of people in the world have ever done: diving beneath the ice to explore the frigid undersea environment firsthand.

They were going to go out diving in just a few minutes, but first I got a quick tour of the station. Chris guided me through a network of long corridors that link the buildings that house laboratories, workshops, a communications center, offices, and living quarters.

Unlike McMurdo, where many of the buildings are made of wood, nearly all the buildings at Scott Base are built of thick foam panels that are sandwiched between sheets of steel. It makes for a very snug, relatively fireproof place to live and work.

However, living inside an all-metal structure in Antarctica has its drawbacks. As Chris led me along the corridors, he kept reaching out and tapping the walls at every turn. When I asked him what he was doing, he said, "Oh, I'm just discharging static electricity. Because there's so much metal around and the air is so dry, you build up quite a static charge walking around here. Touching the walls gets to be a habit."

We ended up in an area of living quarters where bunkrooms lined an entire wall. Each bunkroom had two bunk beds, a desk, a closet, and a few shelves, all neatly arranged in a very small space. The members of Chris's research team were all here: New Zealanders Ed Arron, Mike Page, and Dick Singleton, and Australian Paul Goldsworthy.

While the divers finished packing up their gear, I went back to the main entrance and put on my parka, mittens, and bunny boots, and then I met them all outside. Although the sun was shining, a piercing wind made it rather brisk—it would be even colder out on the sea ice. Carrying dive gear, cameras, and other pieces of equipment, we set out on foot for the dive hut offshore. We followed a winding route through the pressure ridges, crossing over small cracks and slippery snow bridges and between huge, jagged blocks of ice.

Once past the maze of pressure ridges, we got onto more stable ice that was fairly flat and covered with hard-packed snow. Up ahead was the dive hut, a tiny cube painted Scott-Base green. We reached it just as Mike drove up on a snowmobile towing a wooden sled full of air tanks.

The dive hut sits out on the ice, just beyond the line of pressure ridges near shore.

Dressed in his diving gear, Chris is almost ready for his dive beneath the ice.

The dive hole was tucked in among the pressure ridges. It had been kept covered with a sheet of plywood so the surface wouldn't freeze solid. There was a lot of slushy ice floating in the hole, but we cleared that off easily with pole nets. Through the clear water I could see the submerged flanks of the buckled slabs of ice around us stretching far down into the darkness below.

Chris and Mike headed for the hut to change into their dive gear. Over layers of thick, woolly long underwear and socks they put on one-piece neoprene dry suits that fit tightly at the wrists and ankles. They struggled into insulated booties and pulled tight-fitting rubber hoods onto their heads. Next came a weight belt, and then bulky three-fingered gloves that were designed for diving in extremely cold water. ''Martian hands!'' said Mike with a grin.

Each diver then put on a yellow safety harness that had a sturdy metal ring on the front. The last thing to go on was the air tank and breathing apparatus. Two independent regulators—what a diver uses for breathing underwater—were attached to each tank. If one malfunctioned in the icy water, a diver had a backup to use for a safe return to the surface.

Beads of sweat stood out on the divers' foreheads—it was like a sauna inside their suits. Anxious to get into the water, the two men grabbed masks, fins, flashlights, and other underwater gear and walked as quickly as they could over the slick surface toward the dive hole.

Paul, Dick, and Ed were going to be the dive tenders for this dive. Dick helped both divers get their fins on, which is not easy to do standing on ice. Once that job was done, Paul hooked a safety line, called a tether, into the ring of each diver's harness. The tethers were tied to metal bars that had been frozen deep into the ice around the dive hole.

Chris sat down at the edge of the dive hole with his

Diving under thick ice in very cold water is dangerous because many things can go wrong. Regulators can freeze up. Dry suits can leak or malfunction. Unexpected currents can carry a diver far from the dive hole, which may be the only way out of the water. But if divers are tethered, they can be pulled up to safety in case of an emergency.

Paul (center) *and Ed* (right) *tend to the two divers as they prepare for the dive.*

fins dangling in the water. He rinsed his mask with seawater and put it on. Ice formed instantly on the glass, so he took it off, rinsed it, and tried again. This time it was clear enough so that he could at least see out. Ed recorded the time and the amount of air in the tank Chris was wearing on his back. After a final check of his gear, Chris slid into the water. Pieces of ice bobbed up around him. He adjusted his mask, took an underwater camera from Ed, and slowly sank beneath the surface.

I watched him descend into the darkness, a streak of red against a background of turquoise and indigo. His

A diver disappears beneath the surface, while his tender keeps steady pressure on the tether.

bubbles broke quietly at the surface in the hole. Then he veered off, out of sight.

Mike quickly followed, and soon all the proof we had that there were divers in the water below was the occasional movement of the tethers. Paul explained how divers and tenders communicate by giving long pulls and short tugs on the ropes. After that, we just stood around the hole and waited quietly, occasionally stomping our feet to try to keep warm. Paul and Ed kept a tight grip on the tethers, ready to respond to any signal from below. Occasionally a sharp crack would erupt from the ice around us, a reminder that the sea ice was under great pressure here where it was close to land. Once a seal surfaced among the pressure ridges; we couldn't see it, but we listened to it breathing heavily and grinding the ice with its teeth. The wind, too, rose and fell like a breathing animal and each gust whipped up clouds of fine snow that sparkled like diamonds in the pale sunshine.

Far beneath us, the divers were moving through a

With lights and camera, a diver films the inhabitants of the Antarctic seafloor.

crystal underworld of ice and color and life. Underwater, the pressure ridges form great ice caverns that glow with a neon blue light. This time of year, the seawater is extremely clear—divers can see as far as 300 feet or more. Large jellyfish drift slowly along, trailing long tentacles through the clear water. Silhouetted against the bottom

In contrast to the barren land above the ice, the seafloor teems with life. All told, at least 1,500 species of organisms inhabit the Ross Sea. Bright pink sea stars dot the bottom. Short-spined sea urchins slowly bulldoze their way through the sediment, leaving furrows to show where they've been. Anemones, large and small, slowly wave their tentacles through the cold, still water, ready to make a meal out of the small fish, crustaceans, and jellyfish that blunder against them. Three-foot-long ribbon worms snake around the bases of feathery-topped tube worms and soft corals.

From far below the dive hole, a lone diver is silhouetted against the sea ice.

Many of Antarctica's benthic inhabitants grow much larger than their relatives in warmer waters. In most parts of the world, sea spiders are often no bigger than a watch face. But here they reach eight inches in diameter and move about on long, spindly legs. Giant isopods—marine cousins of the pill bugs that live under stones and fallen leaves on land—grow almost as large as a person's hand!

Antarctic volcano sponges are very slow growing—a large one like this might be several hundred years old (above). Sea stars, feathery-topped tube worms, and scallops coexist on the seafloor (right).

of the ice, the shadowy, graceful shapes of Weddell seals cruise past. The water is filled with the sounds of them calling to each other.

On the bottom, here about a hundred feet down, Chris and Paul were working around a study plot that had been laid out on the seafloor. Its boundaries were marked off with stakes that had been pounded into the seabed. There were several other study plots in the vicinity, just offshore from Scott Base. Some were on nearly vertical walls, while others were on rocky slopes or muddy flats. Chris's team was involved in an ongoing study of the communities of benthic organisms that live in and around these different types of underwater habitats. When the divers visited a study plot, they usually

An anemone captures a jellyfish, while long-legged sea spiders scavenge for particles of food.

Anemones (center) and finger sponges are a common sight on a dive beneath the ice.

Most dives under the ice last no more than 30 minutes. By then, divers' fingers are numb and their body core temperatures are beginning to drop. So the divers' time underwater is very limited, even when everything is going well.

It looks cold and it is. When divers surface after a dive, their lips are sometimes blue from the cold.

took photographs and measurements, collected samples, and made detailed notes about the condition and behavior of the organisms living inside the boundaries of the plot.

Through this research, scientists hope to learn more about the different organisms that inhabit these frigid Antarctic waters, their habits, and how they all interact with each other. And by monitoring these study plots for several years, scientists can also detect changes that might be taking place in these fragile and unique undersea communities.

Only 18 minutes had passed when Paul announced that the divers were coming up. Moments later Chris surfaced, sputtering and coughing. His primary regulator had frozen up and was free-flowing—air was streaming out of the mouthpiece uncontrollably.

Weighed down with all their gear, it's nearly impossible for divers to get out of a dive hole without help. Paul grabbed hold of Chris's tank and hauled him up onto the ice. Ed did the same for Mike when he surfaced a minute later. The water on divers' suits and gear froze instantly in the bitterly cold wind. Great lumps of ice formed around the valve stems of their air tanks.

"Well, it wasn't a total loss," said Chris, as he worked the tank off his back, "we made good progress with the measurements and photos before the freeze-up." With lips blue from the cold, both Chris and Mike were obviously in pain now, as blood flowed back into chilled foreheads, fingers, and feet. They hobbled off to the dive hut where they would have to wait several minutes for the ice to thaw off the zippers of their dry suits before they could get out of them and into warm clothes.

Fifteen minutes later, Paul and Dick were sitting at the edge of the hole, putting on their fins and preparing to pick up where the first two divers had left off.

I gave Ed a hand with the tethers during their dive. This time there weren't any equipment failures, and the divers were able to finish surveying the study plot below.

While Paul and Dick changed out of their dry suits, everyone else went to work covering up the dive hole, packing up dive gear, and loading air tanks onto the sled. Mike hauled the tanks back to the station with the snowmobile, while the rest of us retraced our steps through the pressure ridges to the station. Back in the warmth of the galley we devoured fresh scones slathered with jam and cream and washed them down with steaming cups of tea.

Later, Chris showed me some of the photos that he and his team had taken on previous dives. "The sponges are really incredible down here in Antarctica," said Chris, showing me a shot of a huge, flesh-colored volcano sponge that was more than three feet tall. "We've taken samples from quite a few different kinds, and several of them have been found to contain some pretty interesting chemical compounds."

Many sponges produce irritating or toxic substances that ward off predators and keep other sponges from growing too close. Some of the sponges collected by Chris and other marine researchers in these cold southern waters have been found to contain chemicals that can destroy viruses. Perhaps there is a type of sponge growing in McMurdo Sound that contains a substance that might one day be used to treat cancer or AIDS.

There is no telling what undersea treasures scientists will find in the years to come. Almost every dive reveals something new about this fragile and surprisingly rich world of life beneath Antarctic ice.

There are more than one hundred species of sponges in Antarctic waters. They come in a variety of colors, from white and pale yellow to vivid orange and green. They range from small inconspicuous crusts to tall, vase-shaped giants so large a diver could almost fit inside.

These red sponges produce chemicals to ward off predators.

The Wright Valley, part of the Dry Valleys region, stretches out far below Cirque 8. Throughout the Dry Valleys, the landscape is rocky and barren, and there is very little snow. This photo was taken from inside a wind-shaped boulder.

Chapter 8
The Dry Valleys

For a few seconds the wind stopped. There was no sound. No movement. No sign of life as far as the eye could see.

I was standing at the edge of Cirque 8, a bowl-shaped basin cut into the mountaintop, looking down on Wright Valley hundreds of feet below. The valley floor was barren and black—quite a contrast to the glaciers on the steep cliffs surrounding it. Off in the distance, some of the highest peaks in the Transantarctic Mountains stood out sharply against the pale blue sky.

The moment of calm passed, and a blast of wind hit me from behind. I turned to face that wind as I headed back up the cirque toward camp. It was what I imagined walking across the surface of the Moon or Mars might be like. The ground was littered with small stones, chunks of rock, and huge boulders that had been deposited here long ago by the glaciers that once covered these valleys. The rocks all showed signs of having been shaped, carved, or blasted smooth by wind-driven sand. I picked up a jet-black stone about the size of a walnut. The wind had shaped it into a perfect little pyramid, with four flat, polished sides. I slipped this

Ventifacts are rocks that have been shaped and polished by wind-blown sand. Some of the boulders in Cirque 8 have been completely hollowed out by the action of the wind—you can get inside them and peer out through holes in the rock.

The Transantarctic Mountains stretch for more than 1,400 miles across the Antarctic continent, from the Ross Sea to the Weddell Sea. They form a dividing line between East and West Antarctica. Most of the range is buried under enormous glaciers, with only the tallest peaks rising above the ice. But across McMurdo Sound from Ross Island, there is a strange, relatively ice-free region known as the Dry Valleys. The wind roars almost nonstop across the barren landscape of this cold, rocky desert. For geologists and glaciologists, the Dry Valleys are some of Antarctica's most interesting places. The rocks that form the foundation of the continent are exposed here, with little snow or ice to get in the way. These valleys hold many clues about the history of Antarctica and its climate.

wind-shaped stone, or ventifact, into the pocket of my parka, where it clattered against the others I had collected that day.

Through my binoculars I could just make out three figures in the distance. Glacial geologist Dave Marchant and his two field assistants, John Florek and Mark Dubois, were hard at work digging on a low rise about a mile away.

———

We had arrived here in Cirque 8 four days earlier, when a sudden break in a long stretch of bad weather had finally made it possible for helicopters to fly again. Dave and John had left McMurdo first, in a helicopter loaded with field gear and supplies. The plan was that if Dave and John made it in, Mark and I would follow in a second helicopter with the rest of the gear.

Bundled up in our cold-weather clothing, the two of us paced the floors of the Berg Field Center for nearly an hour, waiting for word. Finally a phone rang, and someone shouted "Marchant's made it in—it's a go for you two."

Down on the helo pad, we helped two crewmen load the remaining boxes of food, fuel, and supplies into the helo and watched while they strapped a tent to its undercarriage. Before we knew it, we were soaring across McMurdo Sound, heading toward the continent.

After refueling at Marble Point on the other side of the sound, we flew over glaciers and snowy mountain peaks. But soon the ice and snow gave way to barren rock—we were over the Dry Valleys. The pilot and co-pilot used aerial photos to find their way through the maze of valleys and ridges below. As we approached Cirque 8, the pilot raised Dave on the radio. A faint, crackling voice told us to look for flags they had put up to mark a fairly level spot for landing.

Clearing a jagged ridge, we swooped down into the cirque. The pilot spotted the flags and pointed out two red-coated figures scurrying away from the landing site. He circled once, and then brought the helo gently down to earth.

With the rotor whirling over our heads, we worked feverishly to unload the supplies, and in three minutes the job was done. The pilot gave us a wave, and the helo took off, scattering gear in its wake. It soared away down the cirque, getting smaller and smaller, until it finally disappeared over a ridge.

We were on our own, high up in the mountains in a remote valley that could be reached only by helicopter. The wind toyed with our pile of gear, which suddenly looked quite small out here in the middle of nowhere.

Shelter was the first priority; it was windy and very cold. There were three Scott tents in our pile of gear—

A Navy UH-1N helicopter drops scientists off in the Dry Valleys. Helicopters are indispensable in Antarctica. They carry scientists to remote sites that would be inaccessible by any other means.

The tents we used in Cirque 8 are designed to withstand heavy winds. The sides are made out of double layers of heavy canvas; the entrance is a tunnel of fabric that you have to crawl through on hands and knees.

Rocks, boxes of gear, and coolers of frozen food add weight to keep a tent even more stable in the strong winds.

two for sleeping and one for cooking. For two hours, we struggled against the wind to get the tents up. The most difficult job was pounding the metal tent stakes into the hard, rocky ground. When the tents were all standing and well anchored with stakes, we piled big rocks on the flaps of canvas extending from their bases. "Let's hope that's enough to keep them from blowing away when the wind *really* starts to howl," said Dave, as he added a final load of rocks to the pile.

There was a small Coleman stove for each tent. Cooking gear and several boxes of food were stowed inside the cooking tent, while cots and sleeping bags went in the other two. We stacked the remaining boxes of supplies in neat piles around the camp. There was enough food to feed four people for two or three weeks: cans of stew and chili, tins of oysters and ham, nuts, jam, peanut butter, cheese, powdered drinks, crackers, cereals, and frozen meat, fish, and vegetables. All the frozen food was packed inside insulated coolers, so that the sunlight wouldn't warm it up enough to make it thaw and spoil. The fuel was stored well away from the tents.

The final task was to set up "the dunny"—our toilet. The little red box with its foam seat was placed a ways from the tents, weighted down with a couple of large stones. Sitting out there in the cold wind, without a shred of privacy, was a bizarre experience. But it's amazing how quickly you can get used to something when you have no other options.

Tired, thirsty, and cold, we retreated to the cooking tent for something hot to eat and drink. Later that night, wrapped in my sleeping bag like a caterpillar in a down cocoon, I fell asleep to what sounded like rifle fire. It was the noise of the tent ropes snapping against the canvas as the wind blasted through our tiny camp.

Within a couple of days after our arrival, we had all settled into a regular field-camp routine. The days started at 6:30 A.M. In the morning, the temperature inside the tent Dave and I shared was usually just a few degrees above the outside temperature—which was usually below zero. Before we got out of our sleeping bags, one of us would reach over and light the Coleman stove to warm the tent. Once the stove was turned off, however, the warmth only lasted a few minutes. It was a race to get into frost-stiffened pants, parkas, and boots before the temperature plummeted again.

Over in the cooking tent we'd begin making breakfast. The first thing on the stove was a kettle filled with chunks of ice. All our water for drinking and cooking was produced by melting ice on the stove. Mark and John would take turns hiking across to the upper end of the cirque, where there was a small ice field. Using an ice ax, they would hack out chunks of ice and haul them back to camp.

Breakfast usually consisted of the previous night's leftovers, reheated and served up as a steaming mass. While we were eating, Dave would check in with McMurdo Station on the portable field radio. He reported

The dunny, our truly "outdoor" toilet.

In Antarctic field camps, it is a rule to leave the environment as clean and unspoiled as it was when you arrived. Food scraps, trash, and human waste are all packed up and sealed in containers, then flown back to McMurdo, where they can be disposed of properly.

our condition, and in return got the latest weather up-date and any other important news. That once-a-day radio conversation was our only contact with the out-side world.

After breakfast we would pack a lunch. The menu was the same every day: sandwiches made of peanut butter and jelly spread thickly on big, dry crackers called cabin bread, granola bars, trail mix, thermoses full of a hot drink, and chocolate bars. Most mornings we had to thaw the jars of peanut butter and jam on the stove for several minutes before we could get a knife into the contents.

We filled our water bottles, packed the lunch into backpacks, and then cleaned up the breakfast dishes by wiping them off with paper towels. No water was wasted washing dishes. By 8:30 A.M., dressed in our cold-weather gear and loaded down with an assortment of shovels, ice axes, and rock hammers, we were ready to begin the day's work.

With Dave in the lead, we'd strike out across the cirque and spend the next hour or so head down, scan-ning the ground. Our boots crunched over the stones and gravel deposited by glaciers that had covered this shallow valley long ago. There were ventifacts every-where. Most were covered with desert varnish, a thin shiny coating that forms on rocks exposed to the wind and sun. Desert varnish builds up very slowly. Its thick-ness can be a clue to how long a rock has been exposed to the wind and sun, and not buried under ice and snow.

To me, all the rocks and soils we walked over looked pretty much the same. But to an experienced glacial geologist like Dave, they were very different. Every so often he would stop to examine a particular rock or peer at a handful of soil, noting the color and consis-tency and the types of pebbles it contained. Sometimes he'd just shake his head and we would move on. But

Equipped with shovels, pick axes, and rock hammers, Dave and Mark hike over the rocks high above Cirque 8.

when the evidence on the surface hinted at something more promising further down, the serious digging began. "OK, you guys," he'd say to Mark and John, "let's start digging here." And they would begin excavating the site, with one of them attacking the hard, rocky ground with a pickax to loosen the soil and then taking a break while the other shoveled it out of the ever-deepening pit. It was back-breaking work.

Some pits had to be abandoned when the diggers struck boulders or ice cement—a layer of icy soil frozen so hard it was like real cement. But in most cases, they would keep digging until they created a pit about four feet wide, six feet long, and four or five feet deep. We

Dwarfed by the vastness of the distant landscape, scientists stop for a rest on a rocky hillside.

Mark and John attack the ventifact-covered surface of a glacial deposit with pick and shovel as they begin digging a pit.

could usually see different layers in the sides of the pit, where one glacial deposit overlaid another. The different layers held clues as to how long ago they had been deposited by glaciers, and even what the climate conditions were like when they were deposited.

The positions of the layers relative to each other is also important. Usually, the youngest layers are on top, with older deposits deeper down. But Dave explained that sometimes glaciers picked up chunks of underlying deposits and moved them around. This makes piecing together the history of these valleys much more difficult.

Dave assigned a number to each pit and plotted its location on a map of the cirque. Then he took soil samples from the different layers exposed in the walls of the

Glacial geologist Dave Marchant kneels beside a completed pit in Cirque 8. In the wall of the pit, you can see that a lighter-colored glacial deposit lies over a thicker, darker-colored one.

pit. These samples went into labeled bags that would be flown back to McMurdo by helicopter and eventually sent back to laboratories in the United States for dating and analysis.

The final step was to take photographs of the pit, its general surroundings, and closeup shots of the various

Debating the Effects of Global Warming

East Antarctica is buried under a massive ice sheet that covers 4.5 million square miles, is nearly three miles thick in some places, and contains more than half of all the freshwater on earth. If this enormous block of ice ever melted, sea levels around the world would rise by about two hundred feet.

The East Antarctic ice sheet hasn't always been the way it is today. Since it first formed 35 to 40 million years ago, it has gone through major changes in response to changes in global temperature. During cold periods in earth's history, the ice sheet has been larger than it is today. And during some warm periods, it has been much smaller.

Global temperatures have increased slightly over the past few decades and are expected to increase by several degrees before the middle of the next century. Scientists working in the Dry Valleys are trying to find out what effect this global warming might have on the vast East Antarctic ice sheet.

Some think that the ice sheet might be sensitive to relatively small environmental changes. They propose that as recently as three million years ago—when global temperatures were a few degrees warmer than they are today—much of the ice sheet melted and broke apart. This caused sea levels to rise, so that parts of East Antarctica were under water. It changed the climate so much that trees were able to grow on the slopes of the Transantarctic Mountains. The evidence they use to support this hypothesis comes from samples of Dry Valley deposits that contain fossilized remains of tiny marine organisms and bits of wood that date back to this time. If these scientists are correct about what happened in Antarctica's recent past, then the global warming expected over the next few decades might be enough to cause the East Antarctic ice sheet to melt and break up, which would cause sea levels to rise worldwide.

But Dave Marchant and a number of other scientists disagree with these ideas. For several years, Dave has been sampling and analyzing glacial deposits all over the Dry Valleys. Based on evidence he has found, he thinks that cold, polar desert conditions have existed in the Dry Valleys for at least ten million years. That would mean the East Antarctic ice sheet has remained relatively stable throughout that time and a small amount of global warming in the near future probably won't seriously affect it.

Which hypothesis is correct? It's too soon to tell. A lot more evidence is needed to settle this important debate.

layers. When that was done, the pit was filled in and the area restored as much as possible to its natural condition. Then it was on to the next site.

After a morning of excavating a half ton of rock and gravel, lunch always came as a welcome break. We would take refuge from the wind under an overhanging rock ledge or behind a boulder and then devour our high-fat, high-calorie lunch. On really cold days, we ate quickly and then threw stones as far as we could. The motion of throwing drove the blood down to our fingertips and helped warm up our hands.

The digging continued after lunch and throughout the afternoon. As the day wore on, the sun moved slowly in a circle overhead. Wind was a constant companion. Sometimes we would walk several miles in search of new

Spectacularly shaped ventifacts dot the Dry Valley landscape.

The bright green streak across this rock is a lichen. It can survive the wind, cold, and extreme dryness of these valleys by living just beneath the rock's surface.

sites, often climbing up the steep sides of the cirque in order to get a bird's-eye view of the landscape below. From a higher elevation, Dave would sometimes spot places that looked particularly promising for digging.

It was on these visits to high places above the floor of the cirque that we sometimes discovered signs of life. Streaks of bright green ran along some of the rocks. At first I thought they were just a different type of rock, but the streaks turned out to be lichens. In other parts of the world, lichens grow on the surfaces of rocks, trees, or old stone walls. But Dry Valley lichens live *inside* rocks, just beneath the surface, where they are sheltered enough to survive the wind and cold.

Every day the hiking, digging, and sampling went on until 7:00 or 8:00 P.M. Then we trudged back to camp, our backpacks loaded with sample bags of soil and rock. At the end of an exhausting day, our bright yellow tents were always a welcome sight.

Dinner was the highlight of the day, a time to unwind, give sore muscles a chance to relax, and get really warm after a day out in the cold and wind. Good food is one of the few comforts that Antarctic researchers have while they are working out in remote field camps. We ate steak, chicken, salmon…even lobster!

Preparing the food was a slow process because most everything had to be thawed before it could be cooked. But we passed the time talking, laughing, and listening to music. Yes, music. Dave had brought a Walkman with two tiny speakers and lots of cassette tapes—he was a great fan of oldies from the '50s and '60s. He ran wires from the Walkman to a small solar panel that was set up outside the tent, and in no time at all he would have the tapes running on solar power.

On cloudy days, we had to use batteries if we wanted music. The problem with batteries in Antarctica is that they lose power when they get really cold. Our solution was to heat them up carefully in a frying pan. Once they were warm, they worked.

How strange it was to be there—a tiny oasis of warmth high up in a frigid mountain valley at the bottom of the world, with the wind howling and the midnight sun blazing overhead, listening to the Angels sing "My Boyfriend's Back" and Jerry Lee Lewis pound out "Great Balls of Fire."

After dinner we would talk about the next day's plans and the work that had to get done before the season was over. Dave and his team would spend more than three months in the Dry Valleys before returning to McMurdo. Helicopters would move them from site to site and resupply them with food and fuel. Each day would be spent digging and gathering evidence that might answer some of the questions about the East Antarctic ice sheet and Antarctica's climate history.

"Doing glacial geology in the Dry Valleys," Dave said one night, "is like trying to put together five different jigsaw puzzles at once, where the pieces are all intermixed, the box tops with the photos of the puzzles are all missing, and about a third of the pieces aren't there!" It is challenging, often frustrating research. But I could see that these three people enjoyed the challenge immensely.

On the afternoon of my eighth day, I heard the unmistakable whup, whup, whup, of a helicopter approaching. On the radio that morning I'd learned that a helo would be flying in sometime that day to deliver supplies and to pick me up and fly me back to McMurdo. I crawled out of the tent and watched the helo circle and touch down. Grabbing my gear—now weighted down by a few dozen ventifacts—I climbed aboard. On the way out of the cirque, we flew over three figures standing in a vast field of rock. They waved briefly and then went back to digging pits in the ancient ground.

Windblown sand obscures the mountains behind these ventifacts in the Dry Valleys.

Amundsen-Scott South Pole Station is located at the very bottom of the world on the vast frozen wasteland called the polar plateau.

Chapter 9
The South Pole

The aluminum dome that covers Amundsen-Scott South Pole Station is gradually being buried by drifting snow.

At 2:45 A.M., the streets of McMurdo were empty as I walked along in the bright sunshine, my survival bag slung over my shoulder. But as I stepped into the gloomy darkness of the hangarlike building known as Hill Cargo, there were a few people standing around, all waiting for transport down to the sea ice runway. By Antarctic standards, the wait was surprisingly short. An hour later the ski-equipped LC 130 Hercules, crammed full of cargo, took off for the South Pole.

From one of the plane's small, round windows, I watched the landscape change as we flew south. The glaciers and snowcapped peaks of the Transantarctic Mountains gradually gave way to the East Antarctic ice sheet and what is known as the polar plateau—a high, flat, wasteland of ice and snow that stretches for thousands of miles in every direction.

It took about three hours to fly from McMurdo Station to the Pole. I caught a glimpse of the station as the plane circled before landing. Could anything be more isolated than that small cluster of buildings below?

The LC 130 touched down and slid across the surface on its massive skis, its roaring propellers kicking

The station is named after Roald Amundsen, a Norwegian, and Robert F. Scott, an Englishman, who led independent expeditions to the South Pole in the early 1900s. Scott's party died on the return journey to Ross Island.

At the South Pole, ski-equipped LC 130 Hercules cargo planes keep their engines running. Once shut off, they might not start again in the extreme cold.

There is nothing on earth that can compare to the cold at the South Pole. The average annual temperature is –56° F. During the winter, it plummets to –100° F or worse—the record low is –117° F. At that temperature, if you threw a glassful of water into the air, it would turn to ice before hitting the ground.

up clouds of powdery snow. The plane eased to a stop directly in front of the dome that covers part of the station. A crewman slid open the door and the cold flooded in.

There was a steady wind blowing, and as I crossed the skiway and headed toward the dome, the skin on my face went numb. It was so cold it was hard to breathe. The snow squeaked underfoot. As I got closer, I saw that the dome was half-buried in drifts. The entrance, a tunnel-like steel archway, was actually below the surrounding snow surface. Overhead, a sign announced in large blue letters "The United States of America welcomes you to Amundsen-Scott South Pole Station."

As I walked through the archway, I ran my mitten along the surface of the steel walls, and dislodged a strip of frost three-fingers thick. At its far end, the archway opened up into the dome. Four stories high and 50 yards across, the aluminum dome is simply there to protect the station's three main buildings from wind and drifting snow. It isn't heated, so it is about as cold inside the dome as it is outside.

As I stood looking around, a voice suddenly blared out over a loudspeaker, instructing someone to report to the computer center. Moments later a door opened in the nearest building, and a man stepped out—wearing shorts and a T-shirt! He hurried across the open space and disappeared through another door.

There was a steady stream of people going into what turned out to be the galley. It was now 7:30 A.M., and the place was packed with people eating breakfast, talking, and laughing. It was very warm inside, and the air was heavy with the smells of frying bacon and freshly baked cinnamon rolls. In Antarctica, the galley at Pole is famous for its good food.

I sat down with a cup of steaming-hot coffee and was soon joined by Dr. John Lynch, the station's science director. In addition to doing his own research, John was responsible for coordinating the many different research projects carried out by several dozen visiting scientists. After breakfast, he showed me my quarters and gave me a tour of the station.

To my surprise, I had a tiny room to myself in one of the buildings under the dome. The hallway outside

Inside the unheated dome, boxes of food and supplies surround the buildings. The dome is there to protect the buildings from wind and blowing snow.

During the summer season, space is very limited at the South Pole station, with more than one hundred scientists and support staff living and working there. About half of the station's inhabitants are housed under the dome. The rest live outside in a summer camp of temporary living quarters (like McMurdo's Jamesways—brrr!) not far from the dome.

Temporary living quarters lie beyond a huge fuel bladder filled with jet fuel.

my room was lit only by a string of white Christmas tree lights strung up along the ceiling and over some of the doorways. The darkness was a relief from the 24-hour daylight and the blinding whiteness of the outside world.

The tour didn't take long because everything is fairly close together. Besides the galley, kitchen, and living quarters, the three main buildings under the dome also house communications and computer centers, laboratories, science offices, a meteorological center, a library with a big-screen TV for watching videos, a post office, and a recreation center. But there is much more to the station than just what is under the dome. Running perpendicular to the entrance archway are four other archways that house a medical facility ("Club Med"), a machine shop, a gymnasium, the power plant, and a fuel storage depot.

All of the station's electricity is produced by several large generators that burn jet fuel. A year's supply of fuel—around 250,000 gallons—is stored in nine large rubber bladders in the fuel depot archway. The heat given off by the generators is used to keep the station's buildings warm. Some heat is also piped outside to the snow melter, where snow is melted each day to make water. Water is a precious commodity at Pole, just as it is at all Antarctic stations.

There is more than a year's supply of food stored at the station. Much of it is packed away in several food storage rooms that branch off various archways, but there are also hundreds of boxes of frozen food stacked up all around the inside of the dome. The cooks joke about going shopping for groceries as they walk around the dome and pick out the ingredients they need to make the next meal. Fresh fruits and vegetables—when they are available—are kept in a big walk-in refrigerator. Unlike most refrigerators, though, this one is heated.

My tour ended up back in the galley. As John hurried off in answer to a call over the loudspeaker, I noticed a small monitor mounted on the galley wall. Information about incoming LC 130 flights and station news—along with a weather update on the outside temperature, windchill, air pressure, even ozone levels in the stratosphere overhead—continually scrolled across its tiny screen. At the South Pole, I quickly got used to seeing a minus sign in front of temperatures—outside it was -51° F, with a windchill of -101° F.

Five minutes later, dressed in all of my cold weather gear and with my camera zipped up inside my parka, I headed out of the dome toward the place that early explorers had struggled so hard to reach: the South Pole itself. Today, however, there are two poles to see.

Closest to the station is the ceremonial South Pole. Marking the spot is a red-and-white striped pole, topped with a mirrored sphere, and surrounded by the flags of the 12 nations that signed the original Antarctic

Sitting atop an ice sheet that is 9,300 feet thick, the South Pole station is at a high elevation, and the air is noticeably thin. Living here is like living on a mountain peak, and some new arrivals suffer from high altitude sickness for a few days, until their bodies adjust to the elevation. Walking fast or climbing stairs leaves just about everyone at Pole gasping for breath.

I'm at the ceremonial South Pole, standing in triple-digit windchills. The mirrored sphere on top of the pole resembles a scientific instrument that the early explorers used for viewing and photographing the entire sky.

An American flag and a copper stake mark the site of the geographic South Pole, 90° south latitude.

Treaty. The colorful flags flapping in the polar wind are quite a sight against the dazzling white snow with the dome in the background. I managed to take three pictures before my camera froze up and the film refused to advance.

Not far from the ceremonial pole is the geographic South Pole, where a stout copper stake marks the very bottom of the world, exactly 90° south latitude. About 30 feet beyond it, however, there is a similar stake. And beyond that another, and another…a whole line of pole-marker stakes that runs some distance across the snow. It all seemed a bit mysterious at first, until I learned that the massively thick ice sheet on which I was standing is moving, at the rate of about 30 feet a year. The movement of the ice makes it necessary to re-mark the 90° south point with a new stake each spring. Eventually, the moving ice will carry Amundsen-Scott South Pole Station directly over the geographic South Pole.

The extreme cold limits the amount of time that anyone can spend outside. After circling the pole three times—and thus making three quick trips around the world—I crunched across the snow to the Clean Air Facility.

Remote and isolated, the South Pole station sits near the center of the world's cleanest continent. It's an ideal place to study air quality and other aspects of the earth's atmosphere. When I stepped into the warm building, I found three people at work there, surrounded by computers, instruments, and electronic equipment used for atmospheric studies.

David Gaines, one of two winter-over technicians, was just getting ready to make his daily inspection of the instruments set up on the snow outside, so I joined him back out in the cold. We followed a path across the snow marked by flagged poles linked together with ropes.

David adjusts an instrument that measures the amount of sunlight that reflects off the snow's surface at the South Pole.

David explained that in bad weather, when blowing snow reduced the visibility to zero, he could still make his rounds outside, using the rope as a lifeline back to safety.

Every hundred feet or so, we came upon some sort of instrument set up on the snow. One measured the intensity of the sunlight reaching the ground, another the cloud cover, and still another the brightness of the light reflecting off the snow surface. David made minor adjustments to some of these instruments, making sure never to touch any metal parts with his bare hands. Touching metal at these cold temperatures would be a good way to lose the skin on his fingertips.

Our last stop was an open metal tower about six stories tall—the highest structure at the bottom of the world. We climbed to the top, where several thermometers and a wind-speed detector were bolted securely to the metal frame. The view more than made up for the climb. From this height, I could see the entire station and its flat white surroundings for several miles in every direction.

I could also see that an area of snow to one side of the dome was dotted with telescopes, huge metal reflectors, boxy structures, and other pieces of equipment.

Most of these were designed to investigate things far beyond the earth's atmosphere.

For many astronomers and astrophysicists, the South Pole is like a special window that looks out into the universe. The station is as high as most mountaintop observatories. The high altitude and the bone-dry air make for extremely clear skies. The view through a telescope at the South Pole is better than anywhere else on earth. And because the station sits on the earth's axis, most objects in space circle around the sky at a constant height above the horizon, rather than crossing the sky and disappearing below the horizon like they do almost everywhere else on earth.

Gamma rays are a type of ultra-high-energy radiation. They are produced by exploding stars and other kinds of high-energy objects in the universe. When gamma rays enter the earth's atmosphere, faint pulses of light that can be picked up by light-sensitive detectors are produced.

Two experiments at Pole are designed to detect gamma rays coming from space. In one experiment, two dozen small boxes are arranged in a grid pattern on the snow. Each box houses a detector that is aimed at a particular spot in the sky. Nearby, what looks like a blue plastic swimming pool is packed with photo-sensors—also pointing sky-ward—that have been anchored into position by being frozen in ice.

By tracing gamma rays back to their sources, scientists are learning more about exploding stars and similar objects that are millions of light-years from earth.

Gamma ray detectors are arranged in a grid pattern in the snow. Near them stands the Clean Air Facility.

With all the telescopes and equipment aimed at the sky, a newcomer might get the impression that all of the scientific research going on at the South Pole station has to do with the earth's atmosphere and things far out in

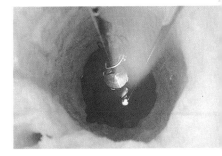

An unusual experiment at Pole involves using the ice sheet itself as a sort of giant detector to track neutrinos. Neutrinos are high-energy particles that come from pulsars and supernovas and can travel through space—and through people, polar ice caps, and entire planets—without even slowing down.

Not far from the station, researchers have used hot-water drills to bore holes in the ice sheet. Each hole is 20 inches across and 3,000 or more feet deep. Suspended in the holes are long strings of detectors that are designed to sense neutrinos passing through the ice. By tracing neutrinos back to their sources, scientists hope to find new pulsars, quasars, and supernovas out in space, objects that are nearly impossible to find with telescopes and other ordinary instruments.

An immense hot-water drill is used to bore deep holes in the ice.

The diaries of many early Antarctic explorers are filled with accounts of brilliant displays of colored lights moving across the dark winter sky. All through the six-month-long polar night, these southern lights, or auroras, are a common sight at the South Pole station. They are most often described as great shimmering bands of violet, red, green, and yellow light that ripple and flutter across the sky. Auroras are caused when subatomic particles coming from the sun interact with the earth's magnetic field and the outer edge of the atmosphere. Using all-sky cameras, researchers can photograph the entire night sky from horizon to horizon, and capture these spectacular light shows on film.

space. But that's not the case. Some researchers at the station study the people, including other scientists, who live and work there.

Dr. Jeffrey Johnson, an anthropologist from East Carolina University, was spending a year learning how well people adapt to living in an extreme and isolated place like the South Pole station. He was particularly interested in studying the winter-overs—the handful of scientists, technicians, and support people who would spend the winter together at the bottom of the world.

At the peak of summer, Pole is alive with activity. Everyone is trying to get an enormous amount done in the few brief months when there is light and when planes can fly people and materials in and out. But that all changes in February. Most of the scientists and support personnel fly out then, leaving only about 20 people behind. These people maintain the facility and keep equipment and experiments running throughout the many months that the station is completely isolated from the rest of the world. No planes will land again until late October. The winter-over people are alone in the fierce cold and darkness at the bottom of the world, with only each other for company. It is probably not an experience that most people would enjoy.

Who will do well under such conditions and who won't? That is the sort of question Jeff Johnson is trying to answer. "Wintering over at the South Pole is probably the closest thing we have to a moon-base or space-station experience," he said. "By studying the winter-over group, maybe we can learn something about the kinds of people who are most likely to do well living in a small, isolated group under extreme conditions." Someday Jeff's findings may be important when it comes to selecting the people who will occupy the first planetary outpost or a space station somewhere in our solar system.

The time I spent at Pole passed very quickly—there was always something interesting going on. After only three days, I left the same way I had come, by LC 130 in the middle of the night. With all its cargo unloaded, the big plane was empty, and as the only passenger, I felt rather odd sitting alone surrounded by all that space.

As we took off, I caught one last glimpse of the station. It wasn't hard to imagine it as a solitary outpost on another planet. The station is an oasis of life and scientific activity in a desert of ice.

The setting sun heralds the onset of a long, dark winter, when South Pole Station is isolated from the rest of the world.

A south polar skua attempts to steal an Adelie penguin's egg.

Chapter 10
Cape Bird

There were signs of spring down below. Great wide cracks now zigzagged through the sea ice, which had been fairly solid just a few weeks ago. Out at the ice edge, where the frozen surface of the sound met the open sea, huge sheets of ice had broken off and were floating free. From the air, these ice floes looked like pieces of a giant jigsaw puzzle, each outlined in blue.

We were flying north, following the contours of Ross Island's jagged coastline. The helicopter skimmed along the foot of an immense glacier that jutted out from the land. Soon great masses of ice would be calving off its sheer front face to become icebergs in the world's southernmost sea. Once we passed the glacier, the pilot swung the helo back over the island and approached Cape Bird from the inland side. Flying low over snow-streaked ridges of volcanic rock, we glided down onto a narrow beach that ran along the rocky shore.

On the left, the sea lapped against tumbled blocks of ice that lay in crazy heaps along the shoreline. In the distance, icebergs and ice floes, now part of the drifting, ever-changing pack ice, sailed past. On the right, black

Ice floes dot the surface of McMurdo Sound.

Every spring over 60,000 Adelie penguins come ashore at Cape Bird to breed. They crowd together on the gently sloping hillsides of their breeding grounds, or rookery, where they build nests, lay eggs, and raise their chicks. From late October until the end of January, the rookery is the site of nonstop activity.

volcanic hills rose up from the beach to meet glaciers and snow-covered mountain peaks.

I waved good-bye to the pilots as the whine of the rotor increased and the helo lifted off. It circled and then headed back to McMurdo, about 60 miles to the south. In the sudden quiet that followed, I heard an odd sound—a sort of low, musical humming. It wasn't until I hiked around the base of a ridge farther up the beach that the source of the sound came into view: penguins! There were penguins covering the landscape as far as I could see. And they all seemed to be calling at once.

Stepping carefully in my big bunny boots, I walked slowly into the rookery, keeping to the open areas

Heads back and beaks pointed skyward, Adelie penguins let go with their characteristic drumroll calls.

between groups of penguins. A few of the birds watched me closely with their jet-black eyes. But most simply ignored me. Like most of Antarctica's wildlife, penguins aren't afraid of people.

I stopped when I was surrounded by penguins on all sides. Now the noise was remarkably loud. The call of a single Adelie penguin sounds like a drumroll that speeds up to a musical gurgle. But when thousands of Adelies all call together, the result is a loud throbbing hum. The sound seemed to roll across the rookery from end to end and back again.

There is nothing like the sound and sight of a penguin rookery. Or the smell. The ground was covered with

There are 17 species of penguins in the world, but only Adelies and emperor penguins breed on the Antarctic continent itself. Adelies are rather small penguins. An adult stands about two feet tall and weighs about 10 pounds.

a thick yellow crust—the matted remains of centuries of penguin droppings. Warmth and sunlight had thawed the surface of this yellow soil enough so it gave off a foul, musty odor.

Everywhere I looked, penguins were sitting on nests made of small stones. At this point in the season, most of the birds were probably males. Male and female Adelies take turns sitting on their eggs—long turns. Once the female has laid her eggs, she leaves the male in charge of incubation and heads out to sea, where she eats lots of krill and small fish and builds up her strength after the hard job of egg-laying. Two weeks later, she comes back, sleek and fat and clean, to trade places with her mate. The hungry male then takes his two-week turn at sea. When he returns, the chicks are just about ready to hatch.

Adelie penguins build nests of small stones into which the female lays one or two pale greenish white eggs. Males take the first turn at incubating the eggs, while the females are feeding far out at sea.

A rather skinny-looking penguin at a nearby nest stood up and stretched. His white breast was streaked with filth. It had probably been many days since he had been in the water or had anything to eat. Desperate for a drink, he left his nest and the two eggs it contained, and walked off to nibble at a patch of nearby snow.

There was movement overhead. A pair of south polar skuas soared silently over the rookery. They had spotted the unattended penguin eggs. The two brownish gray birds circled over the nest. They looked a bit like gulls, but larger and more powerful. One of the pair suddenly swooped down. Hovering above the stone nest—and just out of reach of the sharp beaks of neighboring penguins—the skua deftly plucked an egg from the nest. It flew off with its mate, and the two birds landed farther up the slope, where they proceeded to eat the stolen egg.

That's when I spotted Dr. Gary Miller. He was standing higher up in the rookery, watching the two skuas through a pair of binoculars. I waved to catch his

A south polar skua comes in for an attack (left) *on an unguarded penguin nest and gets away with an egg* (below).

attention. He waved back, jotted something in a notebook, and then slowly picked his way down through the groups of penguins.

Skua researcher Gary Miller and his team of field assistants flew in by helicopter two weeks earlier, when both penguins and skuas were just beginning to arrive for the breeding season. Like the Adelies, skuas come to Cape Bird each spring to lay eggs and raise chicks. Many return year after year to nest in the same spot and with the same mate.

"Did you see that?" Gary asked as he walked up. "Pretty amazing flying. Well, let's get you settled up in the hut." We walked back down the beach and then followed a very narrow path that ran diagonally up a steep hill near the rookery. Perched on a shallow ledge midway up the hillside was a prefab metal hut with three domed tents set up next to it.

The hut at Cape Bird is maintained by the New Zealand Antarctic Program, and at the moment it was home for two New Zealand scientists, Beth Speirs and Shirley McQueen, who were studying Adelie breeding behavior.

South polar skuas are remarkable flyers. They migrate long distances between Antarctica and the Northern Hemisphere—even as far north as Greenland. They are the only birds that have ever been seen at the South Pole.

Many people think of skuas only as vicious predators that snatch penguin eggs, and kill and eat penguin chicks. But the big gull-like birds are more scavengers than predators. They are the clean-up crew in the rookery and eat just about anything, including the carcasses of penguins and other dead animals. And although skuas do take penguin eggs when they get the chance, they prey primarily on sick or feeble penguin chicks. By weeding out the weak, skuas help keep the penguin population healthy and strong.

Piercing skua calls are often heard in the rookery.

Because space was so limited, Gary and his research assistants slept in the tents outside. But everyone took turns cooking, and we all ate together at the big table in the hut's main room, where a row of windows looked out over the sound.

At lunchtime I met Gary's research team—George Wallace, Paige Martin, and Bridget Keimel—as they came back from their morning rounds in the rookery. They too had been out watching skuas, something they would be doing 10 to 12 hours a day for the next two months.

Gary Miller had been studying skuas for several years, trying to discover what factors affect the reproductive success of these birds, and specifically, the survival rate of skua chicks. At Cape Bird, skua chicks in the same nest are very aggressive toward each other, and chick survival rates are low. The question is, why? Is it because parent birds don't bring enough food to the nest, leaving the chicks constantly hungry? Or is there another explanation?

In order to answer questions like these, the researchers had to observe skuas during their entire breeding season, from the time the adults arrived at Cape Bird until the chicks were grown and on their own. The first step was to identify all the skuas in the rookery and locate their nesting sites.

After lunch, Gary led me across the upper slopes of the rookery in search of skuas. Since 1988, New Zealand and American scientists have been banding skuas at Cape Bird, including all the new chicks born each season. By now, most of the returning adults were already banded; they had nested in this rookery before or had been hatched here. The banding system made it possible for researchers to identify individual birds.

"Each bird wears a set of four bands, two on each leg," Gary explained, as we picked our way around

The colored bands that researchers place around skuas' legs make it possible to keep track of individual birds from year to year.

nesting penguins. "You read them starting with the top band on the left foot, then bottom left, bottom right, and finally top right." A pair of big skuas were sitting together on an outcropping of dark rock up ahead. The trick was to move just close enough so that the birds would stand up, but not fly away. We inched ahead. The birds stood and ruffled their wings, but they didn't take off. Through my binoculars I could see the bands around their legs. "The bird on the left is black/yellow/green/blue and the other one...yellow/white/red/white." Gary wrote this down in his book.

Not all the skuas we encountered that afternoon were as cooperative. Many took·to the air before we could get a good look at their bands and make a positive identification. There was nothing to do but follow them, and try again when they landed. And again, and again. This was a job that required patience.

It also required paying attention to skuas circling overhead. If we ventured too close to a pair of skuas

Gary Miller bands a skua chick.

A skua skims low over a group of penguin chicks in the rookery.

Skuas have their share of enemies. At Cape Bird, there are close to 60,000 penguins, but only about 300 skuas. Given a chance, Adelie penguins will kick the eggs out of a skua's nest or trample skua chicks to death under their thick, fleshy feet.

Female skuas typically lay two eggs, but usually only one chick survives. Often the younger chick is killed by its older brother or sister. And any chick that wanders from its nest risks being eaten by neighboring adults. Skuas will indeed eat anything, even other skuas.

that were already defending a nesting site, they aggressively tried to drive us away. "They're gulls trying to become falcons," Gary joked as we crouched down to avoid a set of sharp claws screaming past our heads at high speed. The dive-bombing threats aren't just for show, either. If you don't duck or move off, the skuas *will* hit you with their feet or sharp beaks.

By the end of the day, we had identified about 20 skuas and covered several miles around the rookery. That night Gary and the others compiled all the information on skuas they had recorded during the day. They were also making a map of the rookery that showed exactly where different skua pairs had their nests. Later on in the season, observation blinds would be set up near some nests, and long days and nights would be spent gathering data on egg laying, incubation, hatching, chick behavior, feeding behavior, and eventually, chick survival. The researchers would also band all the chicks, as well as any unbanded adults—provided they could catch them.

During my days at Cape Bird, I spent some of my time helping identify skuas, and on one occasion, lent a hand trying to catch a few unbanded ones—without any luck. But I also spent many hours each day just sitting quietly in the rookery watching the penguins. Day or night, there was always action somewhere.

Adelies are territorial, and every bird is quick to defend the small space around its nest. I noticed that each time a penguin got off its nest, it had to be careful not

A rookery of nesting penguins is filled with nonstop action.

Adelies raise the feathers on the back of their head and round up the white rings around their eyes when they are disturbed, as if to give a gentle warning to "back off."

to step into a neighbor's territory. If it did, the neighbor would fluff its body feathers, raise the ruff of feathers on the back of its neck, and look threateningly at the trespasser with its white-rimmed eyes.

Such mild threats usually were enough to get the intruding bird to step away. But sometimes the intruder responded with threats of its own. This usually led to an exchange of growling, barking calls. If other neighbors joined in, the argument was likely to escalate into a free-for-all of jabbing and poking with sharp beaks. The commotion would keep up until the penguin who was in the wrong place either got back on its nest or walked away, and peace was restored.

Along the barren Antarctic shore, small stones are the only material available for building nests. So for Adelies, stones are a precious commodity. Given half a chance, most penguins will steal stones from their neighbors if they think they can get away with it.

Some stone-stealing penguins were sneaky. They would ease a stone out of a neighbor's nest when it wasn't looking, and quietly add the stolen goods to their own circular piles. Others were more daring. They'd stroll casually through the rookery, then suddenly snatch a stone from a nest and run back to their own. As they hurried through the tightly clustered nests, they'd stretch up their wings, making their bodies as thin as possible to avoid the sharp beaks poking at them from all sides.

Now and then small groups of penguins made their way down to the sea for a drink or a quick bath. Single file they trooped along, teetering from side to side with little wings outstretched. On snowy hillsides, some penguins chose an easier way to get around—they flopped onto their bellies and tobogganed down the slopes.

When the penguins reached the edge of the ice that hugged the shoreline, they never simply jumped right

in. Instead, they stood and gazed into the water, sometimes for an hour or more. Early one morning, I discovered why. About a dozen penguins were standing on a peninsula of ice that jutted out into the water. Suddenly, without warning, a dark, spotted form exploded out of the sea with its mouth open. A half second later there was one less penguin on the ice.

Strong, sleek, and solitary, leopard seals are fierce predators that eat penguins and other species of seals. Leopard seals often prowl near penguin colonies. They

These Adelies are making their way down to the water's edge beyond the rough, tumbled blocks of ice. The penguin in the foreground is tobogganing along on its tummy.

A leopard seal surfaces for a look around. Powerful predators, leopard seals are lone hunters.

wait beneath the ice along the shore and catch penguins going in and out of the water. And as I'd seen, they also can leap out of the water with lightning speed to snatch unwary penguins from the ice edge.

Late one evening near the end of my stay, George burst into the hut, breathless from running up the hillside. He uttered just one word: "Emperors." Grabbing our cameras and binoculars, Gary, Paige, Bridget, and I took off down the path to catch a glimpse of the world's largest penguins.

We stumbled and slid across the jagged tumble of ice along the shore until we stood at the water's edge. Several hundred yards out was a drifting ice floe, moving toward us on the incoming tide. Through my binoculars I could see a dozen emperor penguins standing on the floe. Emperors rarely come onto land. But it looked like these birds would pass quite close to shore as the ice drifted by.

In the open water between the shore and the incoming ice, a group of Adelies were porpoising along at the surface. Moments later they dove beneath the waves and disappeared. Slowly but steadily, the floating ice drifted closer to the shore. The emperors were easy to see now, with the evening sun glinting off their pale yellow breasts. The largest and rarest of all penguins, these birds stand over three feet tall and may weigh up to 65 pounds.

Quite unexpectedly, the little Adelies that had been out swimming and diving suddenly came rocketing out of the water up onto the ice near us. They looked like they had been shot out of a cannon, they were coming up so fast. The reason for their speedy exit from the sea appeared moments later as a large head rose above the surface. It was a leopard seal.

The seal bobbed up higher in the water to get a better look at the Adelies. Dark eyes seemed to be sizing up the distance between predator and prey. After a few seconds, though, the head slipped beneath the surface once more.

The emperors were very close now. We could hear them calling to each other—a nasal, trumpeting sound. As the ice floe drifted by, we followed the emperors as best we could by walking along the shore, struggling over the loose blocks of ice as fast as possible without falling. From the end of the ice peninsula where I'd

A regal-looking emperor penguin stands on the sea ice, calling.

earlier watched the leopard seal snatch a penguin, we managed to get one last look at the beautiful emperors. Then they drifted past us and were gone.

Leaving the others, I wandered down along the far side of the ice peninsula and stood on a low spot near the edge. Far out in the water, a leopard seal surfaced, then quickly disappeared. Thinking it might surface closer the next time it came up for air, I got out my camera and waited. What a great chance for a photo!

More than a minute passed and nothing happened. Then, just as I turned to go, the seal erupted out of the water and landed on the ice right in front of me, eyes bright and jaws open. Large yellow teeth made me forget all about taking a picture. Instead, I took a big step backward. The seal lurched forward, with surprising speed. Another step back—another lurch forward. The next thing I knew, I was scrambling across slippery, broken ice with a very determined—and undoubtedly hungry—leopard seal in pursuit. By now, Gary, Paige, and Bridget had climbed up onto a big block of ice. When I got there, Paige grabbed hold of the back of my parka and hauled me up. The seal slithered right up to the base of the ice block and stared up at us for a long time. Then it tried to take a bite out of a bag of camera gear Gary had left behind. Finally, realizing we were out of reach, it lurched back across the ice and slipped into the water.

Later on, when my heart had stopped pounding, I paced off the distance between the water's edge and the big block of ice. The seal had chased me for 75 feet across the ice. I didn't like to think what could have happened if I had been standing any closer to the edge when that seal came leaping out of the water.

The seal encounter was a dramatic ending to my stay at Cape Bird. It is a magical place, harshly beautiful and teeming with life, but a place where death is always

Lying at the base of the ice block, the leopard seal kept us at bay for several minutes before going back into the sea. The camera bag received only minor injuries.

waiting for the weak and the foolish. I envied the researchers who would witness the wonder of eggs hatching and a rookery full of fat, downy penguin chicks and young skuas learning to fly. As with all the scientists I had met in Antarctica, their research had made it possible for them to see things, and do things, that most people only dream of.

The low sun lights up Antarctica's Mount Discovery.

Index

Amundsen-Scott South Pole Station, 98, 99–109
anemones, 79, 81
Antarctic Treaty, 14, 44, 103–104
anthropologists, 108
antifreeze proteins, 62, 63–64, 71
astronomers, 8, 106–107
atmospheric scientists, 50, 51–56, 104–105

balloons, 50, 51–54
biologists, 8, 39–46, 49, 58–61, 63–71, 74–78, 80, 82–83, 114–118, 122
birds: skuas, 110, 114–115, 116–119, 125. *See also* penguins
boomeranging, 7, 10
breeding colonies, 42, 44, 48, 110, 112–115, 118, 119–122

Castle Rock, 6, 36, 37
chlorofluorocarbons (CFCs), 55–56, 61
climate change, 94

Discovery, Mount, 18, 125
divers, 76–80, 82–83
Dobson spectrophotometers, 55–56, 61
Dry Valleys, 18, 84, 85–97

El Niño, 49
Erebus, Mount, 6, 17–18, 22, 31, 36
exploration, 14, 22, 99, 103, 108

field camps, 25, 39–40
fish, 62, 63–64, 66–71, 79
food, 22–23, 31, 34, 35, 36, 83, 88–89, 90, 96, 101, 102

genetic engineering, 71
geologists, 8, 9, 86–97
glacial deposits, 9, 90–93, 95
glaciers, 14, 36, 85, 111

ice: pack, 111, 122, 123–124; permanent, shelf, 22, 32, 35, 36; pressure ridges, 19, 43, 46–47, 73, 75, 76, 78, 79; sea, 8, 27, 28, 29–31, 38, 43, 49, 58–59, 64, 65, 75, 79, 111; testing thickness, 30–31
ice sheet, East Antarctic, 12, 13, 94, 97, 99, 103, 104, 107

jellyfish, 79, 81

living conditions, 20–23, 34–36, 40, 73–75, 88–90, 96–97, 101–102

marine scientists, 63–71, 74–78, 80, 82–83
McMurdo Sound, 16, 17, 18, 28, 29, 40, 42–49, 58, 62, 83, 111
McMurdo Station, 16, 17, 18–25, 27, 50, 51, 55, 64, 69

New Zealand, 10–11

ozone hole, 54, 56–57, 59, 60, 61
ozone researchers, 50, 51–56, 61

penguins: 60, 61; Adelie, 110, 112–115, 118, 119–122, 125; emperor, 8, 113, 122–124
phytoplankton, 58–60
plant life, 96

Ross Ice Shelf. *See* ice, permanent, shelf
Ross Island, 17, 18, 35, 36, 69, 99, 111
runway, sea-ice, 14–15, 17, 28

Scott Base, 18, 73–75, 80
Scott, Robert F., 22, 99
sea, 41, 43, 48, 63, 72, 73, 77–83, 121
seafloor, 72, 74, 78–82

seals: 60–61, 78; crabeater, 41; leopard, 41, 44,
    121–123, 124; pups, 41, 42, 44–46, 48; Ross, 41;
    Weddell, 38–49, 64–66, 73, 80
sea spiders, 80, 81
sea stars, 72, 79, 80
sea urchins, 79
slang, 19–20
South Pole, 98, 99–109
sponges, 72, 80, 81, 83
survival gear, 10, 29–30, 34–35, 40, 43, 76, 86,
    88–89
survival skills, 26, 27–36, 124

tagging: seals, 44–46, 48; skuas, 116–118
Total Ozone Mapping Spectrometer (TOMS), 56–57
transportation: airplanes, 7, 10, 11–15, 22, 99–100,
    109; helicopters, 22, 86–87, 97, 111, 112;
    tracked vehicles, 17, 28, 29, 31, 32, 39, 43, 64,
    68–69

ultraviolet (UV) radiation, 54, 57, 58–61

ventifacts, 84, 85–86, 90, 95, 97

waste disposal, 23
weather conditions, 11, 23–25, 32, 43, 46, 51,
    52–53, 68–69, 85, 88–89, 100, 103, 104

METRIC CONVERSION FACTORS

When you know	Multiply by	To Find
Celsius	multiply by 1.8, add 32	Fahrenheit
Fahrenheit	subtract 32, multiply by 0.555	Celsius
feet	.30	meters
inches	2.54	centimeters
meters	3.3	feet
miles	1.6	kilometers
pounds	0.45	kilograms

Photo Acknowledgments

Photographs courtesy of Rebecca L. Johnson, with the following exceptions: pp. 1, 2, 6, 27, 28, 29, 31 (left), 33, 34, 36 (right), 37, 41 (right), 47 (bottom), 49, 85, 94, 95, 97, 100, 106, 111, 123, 125, © Rich Kirchner; pp. 8 (left), 15, 42, 44, 46, 98, 107, 109, © Aaron R. Walters; p. 8 (right), D. B. Siniff; pp. 9, 16, 17, 21, 23 (left), 71, 87, 88 (left), 91, 101 (left), 102, © Stuart Klipper; pp. 10, 59 (right), 61, Deneb Karentz; p. 18, Laura Westlund; pp. 20, 26, 36 (left), 110, 113 (right), 115, 116, 117, 118, 119, 120, 122, 124, © Gary D. Miller; p. 22, John Splettstoesser; pp. 25, 39, 40, 47 (top), 48, J. Ward Testa; pp. 41 (left), 72, 73, 78, 79 (left), 80, 81, 83, © John N. Heine; p. 53, Dr. Terry Deshler, University of Wyoming; p. 54, Brian Liedahl; pp. 56, 57, NASA; pp. 62, 79 (right), 108, National Science Foundation.

Front and back cover photographs courtesy of Rebecca L. Johnson. Cover background photograph courtesy of Rich Kirchner.